TWIST IT UP

TWIST IT UP

More Than 60 Delicious Recipes from an Inspiring Young Chef

by **Jack Witherspoon**

with **Lisa Witherspoon**

photographs by **Sheri Giblin**

chronicle books · san francisco

**To my mom . . . who loves me so much and
helped me make my dreams come true.
—J. W.**

Text © 2011 by Jack Witherspoon.
Photographs © 2011 by Sheri Giblin.

Library of Congress Cataloging-in-Publication Data available.
ISBN 978-0-8118-7784-8

Book design by Jennifer Tolo Pierce.
Studio food styling by Christine Wolheim.
Lifestyle food styling by Bonnie Belknap.
Prop styling by Ethel Brennan.
Photo assistance by Shay Harrington.
Typeset in Flama and Dirty Headline.

Manufactured by Toppan Leefung, Da Ling Shan Town,
Dongguan, China, in September 2011.

10 9 8 7 6 5 4 3 2 1

This product conforms to CPSIA 2008.

Chronicle Books LLC
680 Second Street, San Francisco, California 94107

www.chroniclekids.com

CONTENTS

MY STORY

You may be wondering how a boy like me got to write a cookbook like this. I'd probably be wondering the same thing. After all, I haven't been to culinary school, and I don't have my own restaurant (yet). I haven't even started middle school! Here is my story so you'll understand exactly how it all happened.

I was born on April 20, 2000, in Redondo Beach, California, a town near Los Angeles. I have lived here my whole life with my mom and dad and younger brother, Josh. I'm pretty much like any other boy my age: I like to skateboard and surf, I play in Little League, and I hang out with my friends. My life wasn't always this normal, though. In fact, there was a time when I wasn't able to do much of anything.

When I was only two years old, I got a disease called leukemia. It was the type of leukemia that mostly kids get. It was scary when I first got it, but the doctors gave my family and me a lot of hope and told us I had a good chance of being cured. There were lots of hospital visits and doctors' appointments. I lost all of my hair and wasn't able to go to preschool. To help prepare me for school, my mom and dad enrolled me in tae kwon do classes when I was four years old. My leukemia treatment lasted almost 3 1/2 years, finally ending one month after I started kindergarten. The doctors warned us that a relapse would be the worst thing that could happen. If I *did* relapse, I would have only about a 50 percent chance of being cured.

I had been finished with my treatment for a whole year and was just beginning first grade. Life seemed great. I was happy, I liked school, and I had lots of friends. Having leukemia was a distant memory to me now. It was in October 2006 when I had one of my monthly checkups. Even though my blood looked perfect (this is what the doctors test to see if the disease is gone) and I felt fine, my mom noticed something different about me and asked the doctors to take another look. We did a few more tests and then a bone marrow biopsy. The unthinkable had happened: My leukemia had come back!

I was just six years old and had no idea how much my life was about to change. The treatment this time was going to be much more intense than the first time. I would have many hospital stays, each one lasting several days. I had to leave school and say goodbye to all of my friends. I couldn't play sports or do tae kwon do anymore. I lost my hair again—even my eyebrows and eyelashes! That was one of the worst parts of the whole thing, not because I liked my hair so much but because everyone who saw me knew that I was sick.

This time, getting treatment meant staying in the hospital for four or five days at a time every three weeks. My mom or dad was always there, which helped. Sometimes my brother would come, or a friend from school would visit. During my hospital stays, television and video games were mainly how I entertained myself but they didn't always hold my interest. One day I was channel surfing when I stumbled on the Food Network, a channel devoted completely to food and cooking. I had watched my mom cook before but had never paid much attention. This channel took cooking to a whole new level for me. I was totally intrigued! I watched show after show after show. I had my mom write down the ingredients so that when we went home, I could make the recipes with her. I had found something I could do that was totally fun, and even having leukemia couldn't stop me from doing it.

After just a few months of cooking, I told my parents I wanted to be a chef when I grew up. Now when we cooked at home, I was in training for my future profession. One of the things I loved doing was going to restaurants and tasting new dishes. If I liked something, I'd go home and try to re-create it. When I was still getting treatment, my mom, Josh, and I would go to restaurants when the lunch rush was over, around three o'clock in the afternoon. That way, hardly anyone would be in the restaurant, and I wouldn't be exposed to germs and run the risk of infection. (I couldn't go into restaurants when other people were there—my immune system wasn't strong enough.)

It was cool because the restaurants were slow at that time of the day, so if I liked something, I could ask the waitress what was in the dish. Then she'd go back to the kitchen and talk to the chef for me. I was trying all kinds of recipes now. I liked to change things around and put my own twist on them. That's how I came up with my catchphrase, "Twist it up." It's how I love to cook, and makes me feel like I can add my own special touch to a dish. Being home all the time didn't seem so bad anymore!

About a year into my treatment, my mom happened to run into an old friend who owned a restaurant. My mom told him about my leukemia and my goal to someday become a chef. Well, my mom's friend was so impressed and said that if I ever wanted to do a fund-raiser to benefit the charity of my choice, we could use his restaurant—and *I* could do the cooking! My mom came home and told me what happened. I was so excited! It was a dream come true.

I began planning the fund-raiser immediately. We decided it would be for Miller Children's Hospital, and we would give all the proceeds to pediatric leukemia research at the Jonathan Jaques Children's Cancer Center located there (where I was receiving my treatment).

The fund-raiser was a huge success! By the night of the event, we had sold out the whole restaurant—more than 320 people came and there was even a waiting list to get in! *The Los Angeles Times* was there, local television stations, and even CNN! I was on the news . . . *cooking*! My dream to be a chef like the ones I saw on the Food Network had come true. The day of the fund-raiser, December 5, 2007, was the best day of my life.

That night was awesome, but I still had another year left of treatment. I had done it once before, so I knew I could do it again. A few months later, I was well enough to return to school, see all my friends again, and do most of the things that I used to do. I had missed just about all of first grade and most of second grade. I knew going back to school was going to take some adjusting. I hadn't seen my friends for so long, everyone had to get to know me all over again. That was going to be hard.

A few months after I went back to school, my hair started to grow back and I could finally take off my hat. This made me feel better because I was starting to look and feel like my old self again. Catching up at school wasn't easy at first, either—this was going to take some work, too. But no matter how challenging things were, my love of cooking never faded, so by the next December, my family and I organized another one of my fund-raisers. This time, we raised enough money to create the Jack Witherspoon Endowment at Miller Children's Hospital. Then, in June of 2009, I became the pediatric spokesperson for the Beckstrand Cancer Foundation. I was a live-auction item for a chef's dinner at their annual Diamond and Pearl Ball that October. Since 2008, I have taken part in the Profiles of Courage Gala for Miller Children's Hospital each year.

The fund-raisers I've organized and cooked for have allowed me to meet some famous chefs, and I've even gotten to cook with celebrities on national television. I've also done some radio interviews.

Being a chef and cooking has been my dream. Even though the doctors weren't sure how things would turn out for me, I always believed I would be okay and I never gave up hope. Oh, and in June 2010, I became a black belt in tae kwon do. Leukemia had gotten in the way of that dream, too, but it had only postponed it for me.

My passion and dreams to cook have led me on an unbelievable journey. My relapse treatment finally ended in January 2009. I plan to keep on cooking, because it is so fun, and because by cooking, I can help doctors find a cure for leukemia so other kids won't have to go through what I did. I hope you will enjoy cooking—and tasting—all of my awesome recipes and that reading my story will give you hope and inspire you to believe in your dreams, too.

Sincerely,

Chef Jack

Chef Jack

HELPFUL HINTS FROM JACK

1. Before you start cooking, be sure to read the recipe all the way through. That way, you'll have all the ingredients and tools necessary to make it.

2. Always wash your hands before prepping or handling any food.

3. Wash and dry fresh fruits and vegetables thoroughly before using them in a recipe.

4. When you use knives to prep food, always have a parent help you, and be sure to cut on a cutting board.

5. To avoid knocking over hot saucepans, always turn the handles to the side of your stove.

6. Always put on oven mitts before you pick up anything hot, especially when you are lifting things in or out of your oven.

7. Try to stay as clean as you can when cooking. Wear an apron and roll up your sleeves, and wear your hair pulled back if you have long hair.

8. Place the rack in the middle of your oven for cooking unless the recipe says otherwise. When you are finished cooking, remember to turn off your oven or stove.

9. Twist it up on the plate! Use your creativity when arranging food for serving. Drizzle sauces and use fresh herbs to add color and fragrance.

10. Whenever possible, use fresh ingredients instead of canned or frozen.

11. Good cooks know they must always taste as they cook. But no double dipping, please!

You should ALWAYS have adult help while you cook in the kitchen. Be sure an adult is helping you, especially when you use sharp objects and the oven or stove.

KITCHEN EQUIPMENT

Have these kitchen tools on hand to help make twisting it up easier!

 BAKING SHEETS

 BLENDER

 **CHEESE GRATER:** A perforated utensil used to shred cheese and citrus zest.

CHEF'S KNIFE: A large, sharp knife used for chopping and slicing.

 COLANDER: A perforated bowl used to wash or drain food.

 CUTTING BOARD (wood or plastic)

 ELECTRIC MIXER: A standing or handheld mixer with different speeds used to mix batters and doughs.

 **GARLIC PRESS:** A utensil used to crush garlic cloves.

 GLASS PIE PLATE

 **LOAF PAN**

 **MEASURING CUPS AND SPOONS**

 **METAL TONGS:** Used for grasping and turning food.

 **MIXING BOWLS** (small, medium, and large)

 OVEN MITTS AND POT HOLDERS: Thick, heavy-duty cotton that protects hands when handling hot pots and pans.

PARING KNIFE: A small, sharp knife used for trimming and chopping fruits and vegetables.

 PASTRY BRUSH: Used for brushing butter, sauces, or glazes on food.

 POTATO MASHER: A utensil used to mash boiled potatoes.

 **ROASTING PAN:** A shallow metal pan with short sides for use in the oven to roast food.

 **ROLLING PIN**

 ROUND CAKE PANS

 **SAUCEPANS WITH LIDS** (medium and large)

 **SHALLOW BAKING PAN**

 **SKILLETS** (medium and large)

 SLOTTED SPOON: Perfect for removing hot food from liquid.

 **SPATULAS (RUBBER AND METAL):** Used for scraping sides of mixing bowls (rubber), and to apply icing to cakes (metal). Slotted metal spatulas are great for removing foods from liquid and for flipping pancakes.

 STEAMER: A cooking vessel used to steam food on the stovetop.

 STOCKPOTS WITH LIDS (medium and large)

 WAFFLE IRON

 WHISK: A wire utensil used for beating ingredients by hand.

 WIRE RACK

 WOODEN SPOONS: Since they don't get hot, wooden spoons with long handles are the best choice for stirring foods while they cook.

BREAKFAST

In the morning, I just really want to get out the door and start the day. I want to fuel up so I can do all of the things I love—surfing, skateboarding, tae kwon do, and hanging out with my friends and family. Without a good breakfast, I couldn't do any of those things. My favorite breakfast dishes are simple and delicious to make. It's important to be able to whip up something quickly, so you're not waiting around for hours to eat. If you're like me, you want to eat what you love—and then get outside and have fun!

SCRAMBLED EGGS WITH GOAT CHEESE & CHORIZO

  SERVES 4

INGREDIENTS

8 ounces Mexican (fresh) chorizo sausages

8 large eggs at room temperature

¼ cup water

¼ teaspoon kosher salt

Freshly ground pepper, to taste

2 tablespoons minced fresh chives

1 cup crumbled fresh goat cheese

I was almost nine years old when I visited Bobby Flay on the set of his Food Network show, *Grill It!* Scrambled eggs were one of the things he made while I was there. I couldn't believe I was actually getting to taste his cooking. It was delicious! That afternoon inspired me to create a recipe based on what he made. And, of course, the experience made me want to keep cooking and to become a chef just like him one day.

1. In a medium skillet, cook the chorizo over medium heat for 10 to 15 minutes, or until browned and fully cooked. Using tongs, transfer to a cutting board. Cut into bite-size pieces and place on paper towels.

2. Break the eggs into a large bowl and add the water, salt, and pepper. Whisk briskly until thoroughly blended. Stir in the chives.

3. Spray a large skillet with nonstick cooking spray and warm over low heat. Add the egg mixture and cook, stirring occasionally, for 3 to 4 minutes, or until the eggs begin to clump. Stir in the sausage.

When the eggs are almost cooked but still runny on top, stir in the cheese. Lightly cover with aluminum foil and cook for 2 or 3 minutes more, or until the eggs are cooked and the cheese is melted. Remove the foil and serve.

Twist It Up

These are scrambled eggs at their best! The chorizo sausage and goat cheese go really well together. This recipe is a twist on the more typical breakfast ingredients. If you want to play it safe, you can use regular breakfast sausage instead of the chorizo and skip the goat cheese and use Jack or Cheddar instead.

JACK'S SUNDAY BRUNCH FRITTATA

 SERVES 6

 INGREDIENTS

8 slices bacon

1 tablespoon unsalted butter

5 ounces mushrooms (your choice), chopped

10 large eggs at room temperature

1/3 cup milk at room temperature

1/2 teaspoon kosher salt

1/4 teaspoon freshly ground pepper

2 tablespoons chopped fresh chives

1/2 cup frozen white corn kernels, thawed

1 3/4 cups shredded Gruyère cheese

A frittata is like a giant open-face omelet. It's packed with protein and makes for a really filling meal, so I like whipping it up for brunch on Sundays. It looks totally impressive when it's done, so count on wowing your friends when they come over to eat it with you!

1. In a medium skillet, cook the bacon until crisp but still chewy. Using a slotted metal spatula, transfer to paper towels to drain. Let cool, then crumble and set aside.

2. In a large nonstick skillet, melt the butter over medium heat and cook the mushrooms for 4 or 5 minutes, or until tender. Add the crumbled bacon and reduce the heat to medium-low.

3. In a large bowl, whisk together the eggs, milk, salt, and pepper. Stir in the chives, corn, and 1 cup of the cheese. Pour the egg mixture over the mushrooms and bacon in the pan. Stir well to evenly distribute the ingredients, then cook without stirring for 6 to 7 minutes. As the egg mixture begins to set, lift the edges with a metal spatula and tilt the pan to let the uncooked egg flow underneath. Continue cooking until the eggs feel spongy when pressed with a spoon (they will still look wet on top). Sprinkle with the remaining 3/4 cup cheese and reduce the heat to low. Cover the pan with aluminum foil to finish cooking the eggs and melt the cheese, 5 to 6 minutes more. Cut into wedges and serve immediately.

Twist It Up

A frittata is an Italian version of what we call an omelet in the States. Just like with an omelet, you can add in any combination of ingredients that you like. Chopped spinach with roasted potatoes—left over from last night's dinner—topped off with Jack or Cheddar cheese is one of my favorite combos. Or you could toss in broccoli or asparagus. The possibilities are endless!

CEREAL MIX-UP

 EACH MIX-UP SERVES 1

 MIX-UP NO. 1

¼ cup Rice Chex

¼ cup Wheat Chex

½ cup Raisin Bran

½ cup milk

 MIX-UP NO. 2

¼ cup Cheerios

¼ cup Kix

½ cup Honey Smacks

½ cup milk

 MIX-UP NO. 3

¼ cup rice cereal

¼ cup corn flakes

½ cup granola

½ cup milk

This recipe takes a simple breakfast standard and makes it interesting. Mixing up cereals like this lets you achieve the perfect crunch, texture, and sweetness all in one bowl. These are some of my favorite combinations.

 MIX-UP NO. 4

¼ cup corn flakes

¼ cup Wheat Chex

½ cup Cinnamon Life

½ cup milk

For each mix-up, combine the three cereals in a bowl and add the milk.

Twist It Up

Twist this recipe up by adding sliced bananas, strawberries, or blueberries to each combo. And consider strawberry milk, too, especially with the corn flakes and rice cereal. These cereals aren't very sweet, so this milk is great for adding sweetness and flavor.

HOT APPLES & OATMEAL

 SERVES 2

 INGREDIENTS

1³/₄ cups water

¹/₈ teaspoon salt

1 cup quick-cooking oats

¹/₄ cup chopped apple

¹/₄ cup whole milk

1¹/₂ teaspoons brown sugar

¹/₂ teaspoon ground cinnamon

Enjoying hot oatmeal on a cold winter morning is a great way to start the day. It warms me up and keeps me full all the way until lunch. This is the perfect breakfast to have on school days.

1. In a small saucepan, bring the water and salt to a boil.

2. Stir in the oats, reduce the heat to medium, and cook for 5 minutes, stirring occasionally.

3. Meanwhile, place the chopped apple in a microwave-safe bowl and cover with plastic wrap. Cook in the microwave for 1 minute on high, or until the apple pieces are tender.

4. Spoon the oatmeal into bowls and top with the cooked apple and milk. Sprinkle with brown sugar and cinnamon and serve.

Twist It Up

Instead of using brown sugar and cinnamon, drizzle maple syrup over the apples. This oatmeal is also delicious topped with dried cranberries and chopped dried apricots.

AWESOME FRENCH TOAST

 SERVES 6 TO 8

 INGREDIENTS

3 large eggs at room temperature

1 cup half-and-half

2 tablespoons granulated sugar

1 teaspoon vanilla extract

¼ teaspoon salt

8 slices day-old challah bread, each 1 to 1¼ inches thick

4 tablespoons unsalted butter at room temperature

Powdered sugar for dusting

Maple syrup or your favorite jam for serving

Making breakfast in my pajamas and eating homemade French toast makes me look forward to getting up in the morning. This recipe is so good it's hard for me to sleep in anymore! The challah bread is the secret ingredient that makes this French toast the best you've ever had.

1. Preheat the oven to 200°F.

2. In a medium bowl, whisk together the eggs, half-and-half, granulated sugar, vanilla, and salt until blended. Pour the mixture into a pie pan, then soak 2 slices of bread in the mixture for 10 seconds on each side. Place the coated slices on a wire rack with a plate beneath it.

3. In a large nonstick skillet, melt 1 tablespoon of the butter, then add the coated slices and cook for 2 to 3 minutes on each side, or until golden brown.

4. Put the cooked French toast in a shallow baking dish and place in the oven to keep warm. You may lightly cover the dish with aluminum foil so the toast won't get too crispy.

5. Repeat to use the remaining butter, bread, and egg mixture, coating and cooking 2 slices of bread at a time. When ready to serve, dust with powdered sugar and pour maple syrup on top or spread with some of your favorite jam.

Twist It Up

Add ½ teaspoon ground cinnamon or nutmeg to the batter, or just mix it in with the powdered sugar after the French toast is cooked. **HINT: Using day-old or stale bread works best because it is less moist and soaks up the egg and cream mixture better.**

NORWEGIAN PANCAKES

  SERVES 6

INGREDIENTS

3 large eggs at room temperature

1 1/2 cups milk at room temperature

1 cup all-purpose flour

1 teaspoon sugar

1/2 teaspoon vanilla extract

Boysenberry jam or your favorite jam for serving

Powdered sugar for dusting

1 cup whipped cream for garnish (optional)

My mom is half Norwegian, and she used to make these pancakes when she was little. I like them because they're thinner than American pancakes but a little thicker than a crepe, so you can eat a lot of them but not feel stuffed. We made them one morning for some of my friends. We cooked the whole batch, and no one left the table until every pancake was gone!

1. Break the eggs into a blender. Add the milk, flour, sugar, and vanilla and blend on high until smooth.

2. Coat a 9-inch skillet with non-stick cooking spray and warm over medium-high heat. Pour about 1/4 cup batter into the skillet, tilting the pan to coat the bottom. Cook the pancake until the top is covered with little bubbles, about 30 seconds. Flip the pancake with a large metal spatula. Cook on the other side for a few seconds until lightly browned. Carefully transfer the pancake to a platter. Cover with aluminum foil or place in a low oven to keep warm. Repeat with the remaining batter.

3. Spread the pancakes with jam, roll them up, and dust them generously with powdered sugar. Top with whipped cream, if desired. Serve at once.

Twist It Up

In Norway, these pancakes are eaten with lingonberry jam, but I think they taste best with boysenberry. You can make these into cheese blintzes by spreading each with 2 tablespoons of sweetened cream cheese (just add a little powdered sugar, however sweet you like it, and 1 teaspoon heavy cream to 3 ounces softened cream cheese), roll, and serve with jam or fruit syrup.

BEST-EVER BANANA BREAD MUFFINS

  MAKES 12 MUFFINS

 INGREDIENTS

2¼ cups all-purpose flour

2 teaspoons baking powder

½ teaspoon baking soda

¼ teaspoon ground cinnamon

¼ teaspoon ground nutmeg

1 teaspoon salt

½ cup (1 stick) unsalted butter at room temperature

1½ cups sugar

1 cup mashed very ripe bananas

2 large eggs at room temperature

1 teaspoon fresh lemon juice

⅔ cup milk

1 teaspoon vanilla extract

½ teaspoon almond extract

½ cup chopped walnuts (optional)

Even though these muffins are sweet and kind of taste like dessert, they're actually pretty healthy because they are packed with real fruit. They're also super delicious and very addicting.

1. Preheat the oven to 350°F. Coat 12 standard muffin cups with cooking spray or line with paper baking cups.

2. In a large bowl, combine the flour, baking powder, baking soda, cinnamon, nutmeg, and salt. Stir with a whisk to blend.

3. Using an electric mixer on low speed, cream together the butter and sugar for 1 to 2 minutes, or until light and fluffy. Add the bananas, eggs, lemon juice, milk, and vanilla and almond extracts and beat on medium speed until smooth, about 1 minute.

4. Using a rubber spatula, fold the dry ingredients into the banana mixture just until blended; it's okay if a few lumps are still there. If you like, stir in the walnuts.

5. Divide among the prepared muffin cups, filling each three-fourths full. Bake for 20 to 25 minutes, or until the muffins are golden and a toothpick inserted into the center of one comes out clean. If baked without baking cups, let cool for 5 minutes in the pan, then unmold the muffins and transfer to a wire rack to cool; if baked in baking cups, immediately unmold the muffins and transfer to a wire rack.

Twist It Up

These muffins are delicious, but if you get tired of bananas, you can use 1 cup of blueberries or chopped apples instead. Chopped dried cranberries are good, too. If you want these to taste more like cupcakes, add something sweet, like 1½ cups of miniature semisweet chocolate chips.

JACK'S CLASSIC WAFFLES

 MAKES 10 WAFFLES

 INGREDIENTS

2 cups all-purpose flour

1 tablespoon baking powder

¼ teaspoon salt

3 tablespoons sugar

2 large eggs, separated and
at room temperature

1¾ cups milk at room temperature

⅓ cup unsalted butter, melted and
cooled

1 teaspoon vanilla extract

Your favorite syrup or jam, or fresh
fruit and whipped cream for serving

These waffles are super light and fluffy! They can take a while to make, so I usually save them for the weekends when I'm not rushing to get out of the house. When I do make them, I double the batch and freeze the leftover waffles. That way, the next time I want one, I just pop it in the toaster and it's ready in minutes.

1. In a medium bowl, combine the flour, baking powder, salt, and sugar. Stir with a whisk to blend.

2. Spray a waffle iron lightly with cooking spray and preheat according to the manufacturer's directions.

3. Using an electric mixer, beat the egg whites just until stiff, glossy peaks form. In another bowl, using a wire whisk, beat the egg yolks lightly, then stir in the milk, butter, and vanilla and blend well.

4. Pour the liquid ingredients all at once into the dry ingredients, then stir with a wooden spoon just until blended. Using a rubber spatula, gently fold in the beaten egg whites until blended.

5. Ladle the manufacturer's suggested amount of batter (usually a scant ¾ cup) into the preheated waffle iron and bake until the iron stops steaming, about 5 minutes. Carefully remove the waffles with a fork and keep warm in a low oven while cooking the remaining batter. Serve hot, with syrup or jam, or fresh fruit and whipped cream.

Twist It UP

Adding ½ to ¾ cup of blueberries to the batter is great. The blueberries make the waffles so sweet and tangy you won't have to use syrup. For a dessert waffle, add ½ to ¾ cup mini chocolate chips to the batter, top your waffle with sliced strawberries, dust with some powdered sugar, and then give it a nice dollop of whipped cream.

LUNCH

Breakfast may be the meal that jump-starts the day, but lunch is what keeps me going. Around lunchtime, I'm with my friends at school, or if it's the weekend, we're at the beach, in the backyard, or cooking in the kitchen. If I'm making food on weekends when there's a lot going on, I like to serve up favorites, like grilled cheese, but with extras like ham and spicy mustard. Just remember that lunch should never slow you down. It should keep you going, give you tons of energy, and inspire you to feel awesome!

TARRAGON CHICKEN SALAD

  SERVES 4

INGREDIENTS

1 pound chopped cooked
white chicken

½ cup chopped celery

½ cup chopped dried cranberries

¼ cup chopped fresh flat-leaf
parsley

¼ cup chopped raw or blanched
almonds (optional)

6 tablespoons mayonnaise

3 tablespoons sour cream

¼ cup rice vinegar

1 tablespoon minced fresh tarragon

¼ teaspoon kosher salt

Freshly ground pepper

I first tried this chicken salad a long time ago when Mom and I stopped in a café to grab a snack. I liked it so much that I was inspired to make it myself. I'd just started learning to cook, so it took a couple of tries and some experimenting, but I finally got it just the way I like it.

1. Put the chicken, celery, cranberries, and parsley in a large bowl and mix well. (If you like, add the chopped almonds at this time.)

2. In a small bowl, combine the mayonnaise, sour cream, vinegar, tarragon, salt, and pepper to taste. Stir with a wire whisk or fork. Add to the chicken mixture and stir well with a large fork or spoon. Taste and adjust the seasoning.

Twist It UP

This salad makes a great sandwich on multigrain bread with red leaf lettuce. Or you can lose the bread and make it a salad by scooping it on top of a bed of greens. It's a good snack or appetizer with a slice of cucumber on crackers, too.

JACK'S FAVORITE BLTA (BACON, LETTUCE, TOMATO & AVOCADO SANDWICH) WITH HERBED MAYONNAISE

 MAKES 1 SANDWICH

 INGREDIENTS

3 slices bacon

1 small ripe tomato

2 slices crusty bread

½ ripe avocado (sliced lengthwise),
pitted and peeled

Kosher salt and freshly
ground pepper

2 leaves butter lettuce

 HERBED MAYONNAISE

1 tablespoon mayonnaise

½ teaspoon chopped fresh
flat-leaf parsley

½ teaspoon chopped fresh chives

½ teaspoon garlic powder

¼ teaspoon freshly ground pepper

This sandwich is a classic that I never get tired of. The herbed mayo is awesome and can be used on lots of other types of sandwiches, like fresh turkey, chicken, or roast beef. Always use the freshest ingredients to ensure the best flavor.

1. In a small skillet, cook the bacon over medium heat for 4 to 5 minutes, or until crisp but chewy. Using tongs, transfer to paper towels to drain.

2. While the bacon is cooking, make the herbed mayonnaise: In a small bowl, combine the mayonnaise, parsley, chives, garlic powder, and pepper. Mix well and set aside.

3. Using a small, serrated knife, cut the tomato crosswise into ¼-inch-thick slices.

4. Lightly toast the bread. Spread 1½ teaspoons herbed mayonnaise on one side of each piece of toast.

Arrange the avocado slices on top of the mayonnaise on one piece of toast. Cover the avocado with the bacon and tomato slices, then lightly season with salt and pepper. Top with the 2 leaves of lettuce, then press down gently with the other piece of toast. Using a large, serrated knife, cut the sandwich in half diagonally. Serve immediately.

Twist It Up

Twist up this sandwich by adding a slice of red onion, or switching out the lettuce for a few basil leaves. The possibilities are endless, although it's pretty hard to improve on the original recipe.

JACK'S GRILLED HAM & CHEESE

 MAKES 2 SANDWICHES

 INGREDIENTS

4 slices rye bread

2 tablespoons unsalted butter at room temperature

4 teaspoons spicy brown mustard

4 ounces thinly sliced ham

4 ounces thinly sliced Swiss cheese

Grilled cheese sandwiches cooked in a skillet are the best! Add ham and some spicy mustard, and you've got a mouthwatering combination. I make this for lunch at least once every couple of weeks—I think you'll taste why.

1. Place the bread slices on a cutting board. Lightly butter one side of each slice. Turn over and lightly spread the mustard on the other side.

2. Divide the slices of ham and cheese between two slices of bread. Top with the remaining bread slices, butter side facing out.

3. Coat a large skillet with nonstick cooking spray, then warm the pan over medium heat. Cook the sandwiches for about 2 minutes, or until golden brown on the bottom. Using a metal spatula, turn the sandwiches over to brown on the other side, about 2 minutes again. Remove from the pan, cut in half, and serve hot.

Twist It Up

Try this sandwich with some really crunchy kosher baby dills and potato chips on the side. You can also add a sliced tomato and a few basil leaves, or change the meat to corned beef or pastrami, but don't forget the mustard—it's this sandwich's secret ingredient!

BAKED FIVE-CHEESE MACARONI & CHEESE

 SERVES 6 TO 8

 INGREDIENTS

1 pound elbow macaroni

6 tablespoons (¾ stick) unsalted butter

¼ cup all-purpose flour

2 cups milk, warmed

½ teaspoon mustard

½ teaspoon kosher salt

Pinch of cayenne pepper

1 cup shredded white
Cheddar cheese

1 cup shredded Gruyère cheese

1 cup shredded Monterey
Jack cheese

1 cup freshly grated Parmesan cheese

½ cup crumbled fresh goat cheese

½ cup panko (Japanese bread crumbs)

Twist It Up

It's hard to make this delicious mac and cheese recipe any better, but you can add extras, like crumbled bacon and/or chopped jalapeño chiles. Adding sautéed sliced cremini and/or stemmed and sliced shiitake mushrooms to the cheese sauce is scrumptious, too.

The first time I ever watched the Food Network was during one of my hospital stays when I had just relapsed with leukemia. I saw Alton Brown make this dish, and I knew right away that this was something I wanted to try to make myself. This recipe came together after I experimented with different cheeses until I got it just right. You will love the flavor and the crunchy, chewy topping of this cheesy creation.

1. Preheat the oven to 375°F.

2. In a large pot of salted boiling water, cook the macaroni for about 7 minutes, or until al dente. Drain well. Return to the pot and stir in 1 tablespoon of the butter so the noodles don't stick together.

3. In a large saucepan, melt 4 table-spoons of the butter over low heat, then stir in the flour until smooth. Cook, stirring, for about 3 minutes. Gradually add the warmed milk, stirring constantly with a wooden spoon. Bring to a boil over medium heat, then reduce the heat to low, and cook, stirring frequently, until thick and smooth, 6 to 7 minutes. Season with the mustard, salt, and cayenne.

4. Stir the Cheddar cheese, Gruyère cheese, Jack cheese, ½ cup of the Parmesan cheese, and all the goat cheese into the sauce. Stir well until all the cheeses are melted, about 10 minutes. Add the cheese mixture to the macaroni, making sure all of the cheeses have combined evenly and that all of the macaroni is coated.

5. Butter a 9-by-13-inch baking dish with the remaining 1 tablespoon butter. Transfer the macaroni to the dish and spread out evenly. Mix together the bread crumbs and the remaining ½ cup Parmesan cheese until well combined, then sprinkle on top of the casserole.

6. Bake for about 45 minutes, or until browned in spots and bubbly. Serve warm.

CHICKEN QUESADILLAS

  MAKES 2 QUESADILLAS

INGREDIENTS

Two 8-inch flour tortillas

1 cup shredded Monterey Jack cheese

4 tablespoons salsa, plus more for serving

1/2 cup shredded cooked chicken

4 tablespoons chopped fresh cilantro

2 teaspoons unsalted butter

Sour cream and guacamole for serving

These quesadillas are a warm, cheesy delight. I made smaller versions as an appetizer at one of my charity events. This is one of the first dishes I learned to cook.

1. Place a tortilla on a cutting board. Sprinkle half of the cheese evenly on one half of the tortilla, then scoop 2 tablespoons of the salsa over the cheese. Place half of the chicken evenly over the cheese and sprinkle 2 tablespoons of the cilantro on top.

2. In a large skillet, melt 1 teaspoon of the butter over medium heat. Fold the tortilla in half and carefully place in the pan. Cook for 2 or 3 minutes, or until the tortilla is lightly browned on the bottom and the cheese is starting to melt. Use your spatula to flip the tortilla over and cook until it is browned on the other side and the cheese is melted.

3. Carefully slide the quesadilla from the pan onto the cutting board. Cut the quesadilla into 4 wedges, then serve with salsa, sour cream, and guacamole. Repeat to make a second quesadilla.

Twist It Up

You can make quesadillas unique in so many ways. **MY FAVES:** Instead of using chicken, I sometimes add cooked chorizo sausage, chopped steak, or grilled veggies.

AWESOME CHICKEN NOODLE SOUP

 SERVES 8

INGREDIENTS

8 cups chicken broth

2 carrots, peeled and chopped

2 stalks celery, chopped

4 cloves garlic, minced

2 tablespoons chopped fresh flat-leaf parsley

2½ cups fine egg noodles

¾ cup frozen white corn kernels, thawed

2 cups chopped cooked chicken

Kosher salt and freshly ground pepper

The next time you're feeling tired or a little under the weather, you should try this soup. There's no doubt you'll feel better—it's like medicine, but it actually tastes good!

1. In a large pot, combine the broth, carrots, celery, garlic, and parsley and bring to a boil.

2. Stir in the noodles, corn, and chicken. Reduce the heat to medium and cook for 10 minutes, or until the noodles are tender and the chicken and corn are heated through. Season with salt and pepper to taste.

Twist It Up

This soup is really quick to make, especially if you use a roasted chicken from the market. And you can always add more of your favorite veggies, like green beans, chopped tomatoes, or squash.

HEARTY VEGETABLE & BARLEY SOUP

 SERVES 8

 INGREDIENTS

1 cup pearl barley

2 $\frac{1}{2}$ cups water

$\frac{1}{8}$ teaspoon kosher salt, plus
more for seasoning

3 tablespoons unsalted butter

1 yellow onion, finely chopped

1 large stalk celery, chopped

1 large carrot, chopped

$\frac{3}{4}$ cup thinly sliced leeks,
white part only

2 large tomatoes, seeded and finely
chopped

Six 14 $\frac{1}{2}$-ounce cans chicken broth

3 tablespoons minced fresh
flat-leaf parsley

2 teaspoons minced fresh basil

$\frac{1}{2}$ small head cauliflower, cut into
1-inch florets

$\frac{1}{2}$ cup frozen peas

Kosher salt and freshly ground
pepper

A hearty soup will warm you up on a cold day, or lift you up when you're feeling down. This soup is great for lunch or for an after-school snack. My brother and I usually have seconds whenever we make it.

1. Rinse the barley thoroughly. In a medium saucepan, bring the water and the $\frac{1}{8}$ teaspoon salt to a boil. Add the barley, reduce the heat to low, and cook uncovered for 45 minutes, or until tender but still chewy. Drain and set aside.

2. In a large pot, melt the butter over medium heat. Add the onion, celery, carrot, and leeks and cook, stirring occasionally, until the onion is tender, about 5 minutes. Add the tomatoes, broth, parsley, and basil. Bring to a boil, then reduce the heat to low and simmer for 15 minutes.

3. Add the cauliflower and cooked barley and simmer for 10 minutes. Add the peas and simmer until tender, about 5 minutes. Season to taste with salt and pepper.

Twist It Up

Bring on the veggies! Most will work in this recipe, so mix in your faves, like $\frac{3}{4}$ cup each chopped zucchini, potatoes, or broccoli. Instead of using barley, you could use a variety of beans, like 1 cup of either kidney beans, black-eyed peas, or navy or other white beans. To make this a vegetarian soup, use vegetable broth instead of chicken broth.

MOZZARELLA & TOMATO SALAD

 SERVES 2 TO 3

 INGREDIENTS

4 tomatoes, chopped and seeded

6 ounces mozzarella cheese, chopped

$\frac{1}{2}$ cup chopped fresh basil

$\frac{1}{4}$ cup extra-virgin olive oil

1 tablespoon rice wine vinegar

Kosher salt and freshly ground pepper

I made this salad when my family and I went to a concert in the park one summer. We had a picnic with some other families there, and we all brought and shared food. I made this salad and it was one of the first things to go—everyone wanted the recipe. Well, here it is!

1. In a large bowl, combine the tomatoes, cheese, and basil.

2. In a small bowl, whisk together the oil, vinegar, and salt and pepper to taste. Pour over the tomato mixture and toss well. Taste and adjust the seasoning.

Twist It Up

The secret ingredient in this recipe is the rice wine vinegar—it makes the salad taste really refreshing. You can also make this salad by layering a slice of tomato, a basil leaf, and a slice of cheese, then drizzling the dressing on top and giving it a dash of some freshly ground pepper.

ISRAELI COUSCOUS SALAD
WITH TOMATOES & PARSLEY

 SERVES 6

 INGREDIENTS

4 tablespoons olive oil

1 cup Israeli (pearl) couscous

1½ cups boiling water

¼ cup fresh lemon juice

3 tablespoons chopped fresh
flat-leaf parsley

1 teaspoon kosher salt

Freshly ground pepper

3 green onions, finely chopped,
including some of the greens

3 tablespoons chopped celery

½ cup frozen white corn
kernels, thawed

25 grape tomatoes, halved

Couscous can really twist things up—it's a great change from pasta, but like pasta you can make it so many different ways. This salad is great, with all the sweet and savory flavors in it. It's colorful and delicious!

1. In a large saucepan, heat 1 tablespoon of the olive oil over medium heat. Add the couscous and sauté for about 5 minutes, or until lightly browned. Slowly add the boiling water to the couscous. Bring to a boil, reduce the heat to medium-low, and cover. Simmer for 12 minutes, or until the liquid is absorbed and the couscous is tender.

2. Spoon the couscous into a medium bowl and stir with a fork to break up any clumps. In a small bowl, combine the lemon juice, the remaining 3 tablespoons olive oil, the parsley, salt, and pepper to taste.

Whisk together until well blended. Add the green onions, celery, corn, and tomatoes to the cooked couscous. Toss with the dressing and gently stir to mix. Taste and adjust the seasoning.

Twist It Up

This salad is very flavorful and hearty. It has a tangy taste and crunch. These ingredients are good with regular couscous, too. Instead of the lemon juice, you can add rice wine vinegar to give it a little different zing. Serve the salad by itself, or as a side dish with grilled chicken or steak.

EASY CHICKEN & PESTO PIZZA

MAKES ONE 12-INCH PIZZA

 INGREDIENTS

One 12-inch pizza crust such as Boboli

1 cup pesto sauce, store-bought or homemade (page 70)

1 cup shredded cooked chicken

½ red onion, chopped

1 Roma tomato, seeded and chopped

2½ cups shredded mozzarella cheese

2 tablespoons chopped fresh flat-leaf parsley

Making this pizza is fun and easy. Just organize all of your ingredients, put 'em together, and pop the pizza in the oven. Expect to get lots of compliments on this one!

1. Preheat the oven to 375°F.

2. Place the pizza crust on a large baking sheet. With a spatula, spread the pesto sauce evenly on the crust, then top with the chicken, onion, tomato, and cheese. Sprinkle with the parsley.

3. Bake until golden and bubbly on top, 15 to 18 minutes. Cut into 8 wedges and serve hot.

Twist It UP

Replace the pesto sauce with barbecue sauce and create a completely new-tasting pie. Of course, if you like a more traditional flavor, use regular pizza sauce and add pepperoni instead of chicken. Just remember: Making a custom pizza is really easy and fun!

SCHOOL-NIGHT DINNERS

Dinner has always been my favorite meal of the day. Even if I'm super busy with homework or after-school activities like baseball or tae kwon do, the night doesn't feel complete without a satisfying hot meal. If you just keep some basic staples in your cupboards and have some fresh herbs and vegetables on hand, you'll be able to whip up any of my delicious school-night dinners. Don't be afraid to get creative—let your favorite ingredients inspire you—and you'll never run out of new and exciting things to make, even if it's a school night.

RUSTIC HASH

  SERVES 4

 INGREDIENTS

1½ pounds unpeeled small
red potatoes

3 tablespoons unsalted butter

1 large red onion, chopped

1 pound fresh sausages, removed
from casings

One 16-ounce bag frozen corn
kernels, thawed

25 grape tomatoes, halved

½ cup chopped fresh
flat-leaf parsley

Kosher salt and freshly ground
pepper

I came up with this dish one night when I was looking in the pantry and the fridge for inspiration—I wanted to make something different. This is a one-pot meal packed full of flavor and color. There's nothing like making something really tasty using what you already have around the kitchen!

1. Puncture the potatoes with a fork and place in a microwave-safe dish. Microwave the potatoes on high for about 8 minutes, or until they are about two-thirds cooked through (CAUTION: microwave times may vary). Let cool to the touch, then cut them into quarters.

2. In a large skillet, melt the butter over medium heat. Add the onion and sauté for 5 minutes, or until tender. Add the sausage meat, breaking it up with a spoon, and cook until browned. Add the potatoes and cook until they are cooked through but still firm. Finally, add the corn, tomatoes, and parsley and cook until heated through, 6 to 7 minutes. Add salt and pepper to taste.

Twist It Up

This dish looks as good as it tastes, thanks to the red-skinned potatoes, the fresh parsley, and the juicy tomatoes. Use the sausage you like best to make this recipe your own. I like using flavored sausages like chicken and apple or garlic. Sweet Italian sausages are good, too.

MEXICAN-STYLE TURKEY STRIPS

 SERVES 4 TO 6

 INGREDIENTS

2 tablespoons olive oil

3 cloves garlic, crushed

1 pound turkey tenders,
cut into 2-inch pieces

One 8-ounce can tomato sauce

One 8-ounce can chopped tomatoes

1 cup beef broth

1/4 cup chopped fresh cilantro

1/8 teaspoon cayenne pepper

1/2 teaspoon ground cumin

1 teaspoon seasoned salt
such as Lawry's

3 1/2 teaspoons sugar

2 tablespoons flour mixed
with 2 tablespoons water

1 1/2 cups frozen peas, thawed

Steamed rice, or flour or
corn tortillas (optional)

This is one of those fast meals you can make when everyone is really hungry and nobody wants to wait to eat. I always make some rice while I'm cooking the turkey so the eating can happen in no time. This recipe is the definition of good food, cooked really fast.

1. In a large skillet, heat the oil over medium heat. Add the garlic and sauté for 1 minute. Add the turkey and cook for 4 to 5 minutes, or until no longer pink on the outside.

2. Add the tomato sauce, tomatoes, broth, cilantro, cayenne, cumin, seasoned salt, and sugar. Increase the heat to high and bring to a boil, then reduce the heat to low and stir in the flour-water mixture to thicken. Simmer, stirring occasionally, for 10 minutes. Add the peas and cook for 3 minutes, or until heated through. Serve over rice or with warm tortillas, if you like.

Twist It Up

Try different meats instead of the turkey tenders, like chicken tenders or ground beef. You can also turn this recipe into a casserole by mixing the finished sauce with 5 to 6 cups of cooked white rice. Pour into a greased 9-by-13-inch casserole dish, top with lots of shredded Jack cheese, and bake in a preheated 375°F oven for about 30 minutes, or until the cheese is lightly browned and bubbly. This way, you can make it ahead of time and just keep it in the fridge till you're ready for dinner.

FRESH TOMATO & HERB PENNE PASTA

SERVES 6

INGREDIENTS

5 cloves garlic, crushed

1 cup olive oil, plus 2 tablespoons

1 pound penne pasta

2 cups halved grape tomatoes

1 tablespoon chopped fresh basil

1 tablespoon chopped fresh
flat-leaf parsley

1 teaspoon chopped fresh thyme

1 teaspoon chopped fresh oregano

Kosher salt and freshly
ground pepper

1½ cups freshly grated
Parmesan cheese

The flavors in this dish taste so good together, you'll be amazed! Crushing the garlic and putting it in the olive oil the day before is the secret to making this dish exceptional. My mom and I accidentally discovered this when prepping for dinner one night. Infusing the olive oil with the garlic made a huge difference in the taste.

1. In a small bowl, combine the garlic and the 1 cup olive oil. Cover and leave at room temperature overnight.

2. In a large pot of salted boiling water, cook the penne pasta for about 9 minutes, or until al dente, then drain. Return to the pot, add the 2 tablespoons olive oil, and toss so the pasta does not stick together. Cover loosely to keep warm.

3. In a large sauté pan, heat the garlic-infused oil over medium heat. Add the tomatoes and herbs and sauté for 5 or 6 minutes, or until heated through. Pour over the pasta, then add salt and pepper to taste. Sprinkle with the Parmesan cheese and serve right away.

Twist It Up

Using fresh herbs is always best, but if you don't have any on hand, you can substitute dried herbs. Either way, this is a super-fast and easy recipe that's perfect for busy school nights.

ANGEL-HAIR PASTA
WITH TOMATO & BASIL MARINARA SAUCE

 SERVES 6 TO 8

 INGREDIENTS

2 tablespoons olive oil, plus more for drizzling

1 cup chopped yellow onion

4 cloves garlic, crushed

3 tablespoons chopped fresh basil

2 tablespoons chopped fresh flat-leaf parsley

2 teaspoons sugar

3 beef bouillon cubes

Two 14 1/2-ounce cans chopped tomatoes

Two 14 1/2-ounce cans tomato sauce

1 pound angel-hair pasta

Kosher salt and freshly ground pepper

Freshly grated Parmesan cheese for serving

This pasta features my favorite sauce, which is really light and refreshing. If I had to eat the same dinner every night, I think it would be this pasta, I like it *that* much!

1. In a large sauté pan, heat the 2 tablespoons olive oil over medium heat. Add the onion and sauté for 3 minutes, or until translucent. Add the garlic and sauté for 1 minute.

2. Add the basil and parsley and simmer for 2 minutes. Add the sugar, bouillon cubes, tomatoes, and tomato sauce and cook for 20 minutes, stirring occasionally.

3. In a large pot of salted boiling water, cook the pasta for about 3 minutes, or until al dente. Drain well, return to the pot, and drizzle with olive oil so the pasta will not stick together. Cover and keep warm.

4. Taste the sauce and add salt and pepper to taste. Pour the sauce over the warm pasta and toss to coat. Serve with Parmesan cheese for sprinkling.

Twist It Up

For a totally vegetarian option, replace the beef bouillon with veg-etable bouillon. For a hearty (and meaty) Bolognese sauce, add some ground beef and/or sausage and 1/2 cup heavy cream or milk. There are so many ways to make this pasta!

JACK'S PERFECT MEAT LOAF

 SERVES 4 TO 6

 INGREDIENTS

2 pounds ground turkey

½ cup whole milk

½ cup evaporated milk

2 tablespoons chopped mushrooms

½ teaspoon Old Bay Seasoning

1 teaspoon garlic powder

1½ teaspoons seasoned salt such as Lawry's

½ teaspoon onion powder

1 teaspoon Knorr Caldo de Tomate soup base

1 yellow onion, finely chopped

½ cup chopped tomatoes

1 tablespoon Worcestershire sauce

1½ cups panko (Japanese bread crumbs)

2½ tablespoons chopped fresh flat-leaf parsley

3 cloves garlic, crushed

1 large egg, lightly beaten

⅔ cup dried cranberries

3 tablespoons ketchup

If you like sweet and savory in one dish, you'll love this meat loaf. The tangy sweetness of the cranberries combined with the savoriness of the turkey is awesome. It's like having Thanksgiving in a loaf.

1. Preheat the oven to 350°F.

2. In a large bowl, combine all of the ingredients except the ketchup. You can use a spoon at first, but to really mix everything up, you should use your spotlessly clean hands. (That's the fun part!)

3. When all the ingredients are thoroughly mixed, transfer to a 9-by-13-inch baking dish and shape into a loaf. Using a spatula, coat the top of the meat loaf with ketchup. Bake for about 1 hour, or until a toothpick inserted in the loaf comes out clean.

4. Let cool for a few minutes, then slice and serve.

Twist It Up

Meat loaf is great because there are really no rules—you can add just about anything you like. You can leave out the cranberries and the tomatoes and add jalapeño chile, roasted red peppers, or some cayenne pepper instead. Build your own favorite flavor combos around my basic recipe.

JACK'S FAVORITE TURKEY STROGANOFF

 SERVES 4 TO 6

 INGREDIENTS

2 tablespoons extra-virgin olive oil

1/2 cup chopped yellow onion

3 ounces mushrooms, sliced

1 1/2 pounds ground turkey

1/2 cup beef broth

1/2 cup milk

1/2 teaspoon Dijon mustard

1 pound egg noodles

2 tablespoons unsalted butter

1 1/2 cups sour cream

Kosher salt and freshly
ground pepper

Chopped fresh flat-leaf parsley
for garnish

 JACK'S SPECIAL
SEASONING

3 tablespoons all-purpose flour

2 1/2 teaspoons seasoned salt

1/4 teaspoon ground white pepper

2 teaspoons garlic powder

1 teaspoon sugar

1 teaspoon dried thyme

1/2 teaspoon ground nutmeg

I like this dish so much that I decided to make it when I was a guest on a TV show. Bonnie Hunt, the show's host, likes things rich, so when she saw how much sour cream I use in my recipe, she said I was a man after her own heart! It was kind of embarrassing, until I was even *more* embarrassed after realizing that I'd forgotten to add the turkey!

1. In a large, heavy saucepan, heat the oil over medium heat. Add the onion and mushrooms and cook for about 5 minutes, or until soft. Add the turkey, breaking it up with a spoon, and cook until browned. Add the special seasoning ingredients and stir to thoroughly combine. Stir in the broth, milk, and mustard. Bring to a boil over high heat, then reduce the heat to a simmer and cook, uncovered, for 10 minutes.

2. While the sauce is simmering, cook the egg noodles in a large pot of salted boiling water for 8 or 9 minutes, or until al dente. Drain, return to the pan, and toss with the butter so the noodles won't stick together. Cover loosely to keep warm.

3. Stir the sour cream into the sauce and heat through. Add salt and pepper to taste. Add to the warm buttered egg noodles and toss to coat. Serve garnished with parsley.

Twist It Up

Making this dish with ground turkey cuts down on cooking time, but you can also use stew meat or flank steak instead. Just be sure to cut the meat into 1-inch cubes, and then simmer the sauce for 1 1/2 to 2 hours (instead of 10 minutes). You may have to add a little more milk or water if the sauce gets too thick. When you're ready to eat, just add the sour cream and heat through.

FETTUCCINE
WITH CREAM, MUSHROOMS, CHICKEN & PEAS

 SERVES 6

 INGREDIENTS

1 pound fettuccine pasta

4 tablespoons unsalted butter

4 cloves garlic, crushed

6 ounces cremini mushrooms, chopped

2½ cups half-and-half

¼ cup all-purpose flour mixed with ¼ cup water

1½ cups freshly grated Parmesan cheese

1 cup frozen peas, thawed

1 cup shredded cooked chicken

Kosher salt and freshly ground pepper

Trust me: These ingredients are totally delicious together. I cooked this dish one night with chef Fabio Viviani when my family and I were visiting him at his restaurant in Moorpark, California. He has an exhibition kitchen there, so everyone in the restaurant got to watch us. Cooking with him was kind of like being onstage—and so much fun!

1. In a large pot of salted boiling water, cook the fettuccine for 5 to 7 minutes, or until al dente. Drain and return to the pot. Toss with 2 tablespoons of the butter to keep the noodles from sticking together. Cover loosely to keep warm.

2. While the noodles are cooking, in a large saucepan over medium heat, melt the remaining 2 tablespoons butter. Add the garlic and sauté for 1 minute. Add the mushrooms and cook for 3 to 4 minutes, or until tender. Gradually add the half-and-half and cook, stirring occasionally, for 4 or 5 minutes or until hot and slightly bubbly. The sauce will be thin. Gradually stir in the flour and water mixture and cook, stirring frequently, until thickened.

3. Add 1 cup of the Parmesan cheese, then stir constantly for 2 to 3 minutes, or until the cheese is melted. Finally, add the peas and chicken and cook for 5 or 6 minutes, or until the ingredients are heated through. Season to taste with salt and pepper. Toss with the cooked fettuccine, then serve topped with the remaining ½ cup Parmesan.

Twist It Up

Cream sauce is one of my favorites for pasta. It's richer than tomato sauces, so I make it maybe once or twice a month. I like using spinach fettuccine, too. It adds flavor and gives a splash of color to the dish.

ORZO WITH TOMATO & MUSHROOMS

 SERVES 6

 INGREDIENTS

¼ cup olive oil, plus more
for drizzling

1 red onion, finely chopped

4 cloves garlic, crushed

1 pound mushrooms,
thinly sliced

5 Roma tomatoes, seeded
and chopped

3 tablespoons chopped fresh
flat-leaf parsley

2 teaspoons sugar

1 teaspoon kosher salt

¼ teaspoon freshly ground pepper

1¾ cups beef broth

2 tablespoons flour mixed
with 2 tablespoons water

12 ounces orzo pasta

Freshly grated Parmesan cheese
for sprinkling

I love making orzo. It looks like rice but tastes like pasta. Surprisingly, there don't seem to be many recipes that call for it. This dish is rich and delicious and goes perfectly with this type of pasta. It's vegetarian but still very satisfying.

1. In a medium, heavy saucepan, heat the ¼ cup olive oil over medium heat. Add the onion and sauté for 3 minutes, or until translucent. Add the garlic and sauté for 1 minute. Add the mushrooms, tomatoes, parsley, sugar, salt, and pepper, and cook for 10 minutes. Add the beef broth and bring to a boil, then reduce the heat to a simmer. Add the flour and water mixture and cook for 10 minutes, stirring occasionally.

2. While the sauce is simmering, cook the orzo in a large pot of salted water for about 8 minutes, or until al dente. Drain, then pour into a large serving bowl and lightly drizzle with olive oil.

3. Pour the sauce over the orzo, toss to coat, and sprinkle with the Parmesan cheese. Serve hot.

Twist It Up

This sauce is terrific with pasta, but you can also serve it as a topping for grilled chicken or steak. With roasted potatoes on the side, you'll have an awesome dinner everyone will love.

IRRESISTIBLE CHICKEN TACOS

 MAKES 12 TACOS

 INGREDIENTS

¼ cup olive oil

1 yellow onion, finely chopped

4 cloves garlic, crushed

2 pounds shredded cooked chicken

1 teaspoon chili powder

1 teaspoon ground cumin

2 teaspoons Knorr Caldo de Tomate soup base

½ cup chopped fresh cilantro

One 14½ ounce can chopped tomatoes with juice

Kosher salt and freshly ground pepper

(continued)

The chicken filling in these tacos is so tasty, I like eating it all by itself. When it's simmering on the stove, I always sneak in lots of taste tests. Sometimes my mom gets a little mad, because she says we won't have any left for the actual tacos. I just make sure we cook a lot so that never happens.

1. In a large skillet, heat the oil over medium heat. Add the yellow onion and cook for 3 minutes, or until translucent. Add the garlic and sauté for 1 minute. Add the chicken, chili powder, cumin, soup base, ¼ cup of the chopped cilantro, and all of the tomatoes and juice. Bring to a simmer and cook, stirring occasionally, for 20 minutes, adding water if necessary to keep from scorching. Add salt and pepper to taste.

2. While the filling is simmering, preheat the oven to 275°F. Place the taco shells on a baking sheet and bake for 3 minutes, or until heated.

3. Using tongs, divide the shells among plates. Fill each warm taco shell with the chicken mixture, then top with some of the cheese, red onion (if desired), sour cream, guacamole, and lettuce. Sprinkle the tacos with the remaining cilantro and serve.

continued >>>>>

12 crunchy taco shells

2 cups shredded Cheddar cheese

1 cup chopped red onion (optional)

1 cup sour cream

1 cup guacamole

1 cup shredded romaine lettuce

Twist It Up

The chicken filling in this recipe can also be used for burritos. Just warm up some flour tortillas and add the chicken, some shredded cheese, and lettuce and wrap away. To make it a "wet" burrito, heat a can of enchilada sauce and pour $1/4$ cup over the top of each burrito, then generously sprinkle with some shredded Mexican cheese and melt in a preheated 375°F oven for 4 to 5 minutes—it's delicious!

CREAMY PESTO PASTA

 SERVES 4 TO 6

 CREAMY PESTO SAUCE

½ cup pine nuts

3 cups firmly packed fresh basil leaves

½ cup freshly grated Parmesan cheese

4 cloves garlic

1 cup extra-virgin olive oil, plus more for drizzling

¼ teaspoon kosher salt

Freshly ground pepper

1½ cups heavy cream

 INGREDIENTS

1 pound fusilli pasta

The flavors of the basil and garlic paired with the pine nuts are so awesome. This is a great flavor change from the typical tomato-based sauces. I usually make two batches at a time so I can freeze some. Then, the next time I want to make pesto pasta, I can make it in a snap.

1. For the pesto sauce: Preheat the oven to 350°F. Spread the pine nuts on a rimmed baking sheet and toast in the oven, turning occasionally, for 5 to 6 minutes, or until golden brown. Pour into a bowl and let cool.

2. In a food processor or blender, combine the toasted pine nuts, basil, cheese, and garlic. Process until finely chopped. With the machine running, gradually add the olive oil and process until smooth. Season with the salt and pepper to taste.

3. In a large sauté pan, gently boil the cream until it begins to reduce, about 5 minutes. Gradually stir in the basil mixture and cook until it is incorporated into the cream. Set aside and keep warm.

4. While the cream is reducing, in a large pot of salted boiling water, cook the pasta for 8 to 10 minutes, or until al dente. Toss the pasta with the sauce and dizzle with olive oil, if desired. Serve and enjoy!

Twist It Up

This sauce is delicious, rich, and creamy. For a lighter version, omit step 3 and leave out the cream. To add color and more flavor, try adding some chopped sun-dried or Roma tomatoes.

WEEKEND MEALS

If you're like me, you love weekends. Being able to sleep in is awesome! The weekends are great because you can do all the fun things you never have time for during the week, like surfing, swimming, or just hanging out with friends. My weekend recipes are bigger, heartier dishes, perfect for serving when your friends come over. And the best part? If you end up with leftovers, these recipes taste even better the next day.

WHITE CHICKEN CHILI

SERVES 6 TO 8

INGREDIENTS

2 tablespoons extra-virgin olive oil

1 yellow onion, finely chopped

1 yellow bell pepper, seeded, deveined, and finely chopped

1 jalapeño chile, seeded and minced

4 cloves garlic, crushed

2½ teaspoons ground cumin

½ teaspoon Tiger Sauce or other hot sauce

1½ teaspoons kosher salt

½ teaspoon ground white pepper

3¼ cups milk

One 14¾-ounce can creamed corn

One 15¼-ounce can white corn kernels, drained

Two 15-ounce cans cannellini (white kidney) beans, drained and rinsed

1 whole roast chicken, skinned, boned, and meat shredded

1 cup chopped red onion (optional)

1 cup chopped fresh cilantro

2 cups shredded Cheddar cheese

I'd never heard of white chili before I tried some at a friend's house one Halloween a few years ago. It was so good, I asked my mom if we could try making some together. This recipe is savory, creamy, and (yes!) sweet, with a little spicy kick. I really like it.

1. In a large stockpot, heat the olive oil over medium heat. Add the yellow onion, bell pepper, and jalapeño and sauté for 3 minutes. Add the garlic and sauté for 1 minute. Add the cumin, Tiger Sauce, salt, pepper, milk, creamed corn, corn kernels, and beans, stirring until the ingredients are combined. Bring to a boil, then reduce the heat to a simmer and cook for about 10 minutes.

2. Add the shredded chicken and heat through. Taste and adjust the seasoning. Divide among individual bowls and garnish with red onion (if you like), cilantro, and cheese.

Twist It Up

This dish tastes like a Mexican chicken stew. It's a great one-pot meal, and perfect for serving at get-togethers with family and friends. Just leave the pot on the stove and let your guests help themselves.

ROCKIN' CHILI

 SERVES 6 TO 8

 INGREDIENTS

2 tablespoons olive oil

2 yellow onions, finely chopped

6 cloves garlic, minced

2½ pounds ground turkey

1 tablespoon chili powder

2 tablespoons ground cumin

1 tablespoon seasoned salt
such as Lawry's

½ teaspoon cayenne pepper

1 teaspoon dried oregano

½ teaspoon ground cinnamon

¼ cup packed brown sugar

1½ teaspoons unsweetened
cocoa powder

(continued)

One Memorial Day, I decided to enter a chili cook-off at a friend's house. This was going to be extra challenging because I'd never cooked chili before. I researched lots of different recipes and asked other people how they made theirs before I came up with this one. I ended up getting second place, which wasn't too bad, considering that the winner was a student at the Cordon Bleu culinary school! I guess it wouldn't have looked right losing to a nine-year-old, which is how old I was at the time.

1. In a large stockpot, heat the olive oil over medium heat. Add the yellow onions and cook the onion for 3 minutes, or until translucent. Add the garlic and cook for 1 minute. Add the ground turkey and lightly brown, breaking it up with a spoon. Stir in the chili powder, cumin, seasoned salt, cayenne, oregano, cinnamon, brown sugar, and cocoa.

2. Add the pinto beans, black beans, chopped tomatoes and juice, and tomato paste and cook until bubbly. Add the white corn and simmer for 45 minutes, stirring occasionally. Serve in bowls, generously garnished with red onion (if you like), cilantro, Cheddar cheese, and sour cream.

continued >>>>>

Three 14 1/2-ounce cans pinto beans, undrained

One 14 1/2-ounce can black beans, undrained

Two 14 1/2-ounce cans chopped tomatoes with juice

One 6-ounce can tomato paste

One 16-ounce package frozen white corn kernels

1 cup finely chopped red onion (optional)

1 cup chopped fresh cilantro

1 cup shredded Cheddar cheese

1 cup sour cream

Twist It Up

This chili is traditional in style and rich in flavor. If you want to twist it up, you could use ground beef or stew meat instead of the ground turkey. If you use stew meat, you will have to let it simmer longer for the meat to get tender, though, 1 1/2 to 2 hours.

JACK'S HOME-STYLE CRISPY FRIED CHICKEN

 SERVES 4 TO 6

 INGREDIENTS

2 cups buttermilk at room temperature

1/2 teaspoon Tabasco sauce

1/2 teaspoon kosher salt

6 chicken legs

6 chicken thighs

1 teaspoon seasoned salt such as Lawry's

2 tablespoons onion powder

1 tablespoon garlic powder

2 tablespoons dried parsley flakes

2 tablespoons Old Bay Seasoning

1 teaspoon freshly ground pepper

1 1/2 cups all-purpose flour

2 cups canola oil

This is the best homemade fried chicken, if I may say so! The secret to this dish is soaking the chicken in the buttermilk and Tabasco—it makes the chicken super moist. Using a cast-iron pan will give you the best results, because it keeps the oil really hot, making the chicken even crispier.

1. In a 9-by-13-inch glass baking dish, combine the buttermilk and Tabasco sauce. Stir to blend. Season the chicken with the kosher salt and add to the baking dish. Turn the chicken to coat, then cover the dish with plastic wrap and refrigerate for at least 1 hour or overnight, turning once.

2. In a shallow baking dish, combine the seasoned salt, onion powder, garlic powder, parsley, Old Bay Seasoning, pepper, and flour. Stir with a whisk to blend well. Remove a piece of chicken from the buttermilk mixture, shake off the excess, and dredge in the flour mixture, turning to coat evenly. Transfer to a wire rack set over a rimmed baking sheet. Repeat with the remaining chicken.

3. In a 12-inch cast-iron skillet, heat the oil over medium-high heat. (The oil gets really hot, so make sure there is a grown-up to help you fry the chicken!) When the oil is shimmering hot, add half of the chicken pieces, skin side down, and cover. Cook until golden brown, about 5 minutes. Turn the chicken, then cover once more and reduce the heat to medium. Cook for another 5 minutes. Reduce the heat to medium-low, turn the chicken again, and cook until it is cooked all the way through, 3 to 5 minutes more. Using tongs, transfer to paper towels to drain for a minute or two, then transfer to a baking dish and keep warm in a low oven. Repeat to cook the remaining chicken.

Twist It Up

For a little more kick, add 1/8 to 1/4 teaspoon cayenne pepper to the flour mixture. This chicken tastes great hot or cold, so it's perfect to take to the beach or on a picnic.

SUPER SPINACH & CHEESE ENCHILADAS

 **MAKES 16 ENCHILADAS;
SERVES 6 TO 8**

 ENCHILADA SAUCE

2 tablespoons olive oil

½ yellow onion, finely chopped

4 cloves garlic, minced

One 28-ounce can mild
enchilada sauce

2 tablespoons chopped fresh
cilantro

1 beef bouillon cube

Kosher salt and freshly
ground pepper

ENCHILADAS

3½ cups grated Monterey
Jack cheese

½ yellow onion, finely chopped

4 cloves garlic, minced

2 tablespoons minced fresh cilantro

One 10-ounce package frozen finely
chopped spinach, thawed, drained,
and squeezed dry by handfuls

1 cup canola oil

16 corn tortillas

½ cup sharp Cheddar cheese

Whenever we go to my favorite Mexican restaurant, I always order these spinach and cheese enchiladas. Once I got into cooking and had a little experience under my belt, I wanted to try to make them myself. This recipe is terrific and meets my standards to be called "super" enchiladas!

1.   Preheat the oven to 375°F.

2.   For the sauce: In a large sauté pan, heat the olive oil over medium heat. Add the onion and sauté for 3 minutes, or until translucent. Add the garlic and sauté for 1 minute. Add the canned sauce, cilantro, and bouillon cube. Bring to a boil, then reduce the heat to a simmer and cook for 10 minutes. Season with salt and pepper to taste.

3.   For the enchiladas: In a large bowl, combine 2½ cups of the Monterey Jack cheese, the onion, garlic, cilantro, and spinach. Stir well to thoroughly combine the ingredients and set aside.

4.   In a large skillet, heat the canola oil over medium-high heat. Using tongs, dip a tortilla in the hot oil for 2 to 3 seconds on each side. Transfer to paper towels to drain. Repeat with the remaining tortillas, one at a time.

5.   Evenly coat the bottom of a 9-by-13-inch baking dish with ½ cup of the enchilada sauce. Using tongs, dip a tortilla in the enchilada sauce to lightly coat it on both sides. Transfer the tortilla to a plate. Spoon about 2 tablespoons of the filling in a line down the middle of the tortilla. Roll up the tortilla and place, seam-side down, in the baking dish. Repeat until all of the tortillas are filled. Pour the remaining sauce over the enchiladas. Sprinkle with the remaining Monterey Jack cheese and the sharp Cheddar cheese. Cover with aluminum foil and bake for 15 to 20 minutes or until the enchiladas are hot and steaming. Remove the foil and bake for 5 minutes more, until the cheese is melted and slightly brown. Let stand for 5 minutes before serving.

YUMMIEST EGGPLANT PARMESAN

  SERVES 6 TO 8

INGREDIENTS

7 cups Marinara Sauce (page 88)

2 cups dried bread crumbs

1 teaspoon kosher salt

4 teaspoons garlic powder

1 teaspoon dried basil

2 cups all-purpose flour

4 eggs at room temperature

1/2 cup water

2 eggplants, cut crosswise into 1/4-inch-thick slices

3 tablespoons olive oil

1 pound provolone cheese, thinly sliced

1/2 cup freshly grated Parmesan cheese

I made this dish at one of my "Cooking up Dreams" fund-raisers. I wrote the menu to include all of my favorite dishes, and this one was at the top of my list. I know eggplant isn't always the most popular vegetable, but this recipe will win over even the pickiest of eaters.

1. Preheat the oven to 375°F.

2. In a large saucepan, heat the marinara sauce over medium heat. Meanwhile, in a pie pan or shallow baking dish, combine the bread crumbs, salt, garlic powder, and basil. Stir with a whisk to blend. Put the flour in another pie pan. In a large bowl, whisk together the eggs and water until blended. Dip an eggplant slice in the egg mixture, dredge in the flour, and then in the bread crumb mixture, coating both sides evenly each time. Repeat with all the eggplant slices and place on a wire rack set over a rimmed baking sheet.

3. In a large skillet, heat the olive oil over medium heat. Add the eggplant slices and brown, in batches, cooking them for 3 to 4 minutes on each side. Using a slotted metal spatula, transfer to paper towels to drain.

4. Arrange a layer of eggplant in a 9-by-13-inch baking dish. Spoon one-third of the sauce evenly over it and top with one-third of the provolone. Repeat with two more layers of eggplant, sauce, and provolone. Top the final layer with the Parmesan.

5. Bake, uncovered, for 20 to 25 minutes, or until the cheese has melted and is slightly browned and bubbly.

OLD-FASHIONED POT ROAST
WITH GRAVY

 SERVES 6 TO 8

 INGREDIENTS

1 cup all-purpose flour,
plus 6 tablespoons

One 4- to 5-pound boneless
beef chuck or rump roast

2 tablespoons, plus ½ cup (1 stick)
unsalted butter at room temperature

2 tablespoons olive oil

4 cloves garlic, minced

4 cups beef broth

1 tablespoon Grill Mates Montreal
Steak Seasoning

½ teaspoon kosher salt

¼ teaspoon cayenne pepper

½ teaspoon freshly ground
black pepper

This dish takes all afternoon to cook, but it's worth it: The whole house smells great! One time when I was making it, the front door was open. I heard a holler as the mailman came by to drop off the mail. He was hollering because he just realized that all the cooking aromas were coming from our house. He came by to thank me for making his route so enjoyable that day, and for making the whole neighborhood smell good.

1. Preheat the oven to 350°F.

2. Rub the 1 cup flour onto all sides of the roast, brushing off any excess. In a large, heavy, ovenproof pot, melt the 2 tablespoons butter with the olive oil over medium-high heat. Add the meat and brown well on all sides. Add the garlic and cook for 1 minute. Add the broth, steak seasoning, salt, cayenne, black pepper, cumin, parsley, and basil. Bring to a boil, cover, place in the oven, and bake for 1½ hours.

3. Remove from the oven and add the onions, carrots, and potatoes. Cover and bake until the vegetables are fork-tender, about 1 hour. Add

the peas and return to the oven for 5 minutes to heat through.

4. Using two spoons, transfer the meat to a platter. Using a slotted spoon, transfer the vegetables to the platter, cover loosely with aluminum foil, and set aside. Using a large spoon, skim the fat from the drippings in the pan. Pour off 2 cups of the drippings (use a 16-ounce glass measuring cup) and set them aside.

5. In a large skillet, melt the ½ cup butter over medium heat. Gradually whisk in the 6 tablespoons flour. Cook, whisking constantly, until the mixture (this is called a "roux") turns a deep golden color.

½ teaspoon ground cumin

1 teaspoon dried parsley

1 teaspoon dried basil

12 pearl onions, peeled

2 cups baby carrots

10 baby red potatoes,
cut into quarters

One 16-ounce package petite
frozen peas

6. Gradually whisk the defatted drippings into the roux and cook until thickened, about 5 minutes. For thinner gravy, add more drippings. Taste and adjust the seasoning. Pour into a gravy boat. Slice the roast at the table and serve with the vegetables.

Twist It Up

This is probably the biggest dish I have ever made. It has a lot of steps, but it is worth the work. I love the gravy, but getting it right is the hardest part. Making the roux the right consistency and color is key. You also have to simmer the gravy for a while to make sure you cook out the flour taste. Mom gave me some helpful tips like adding a little water or milk to smooth out the flavor or adding some sugar if it's too bitter.

FAVORITE SPINACH & CHEESE STUFFED SHELLS
WITH MARINARA SAUCE

 MAKES ABOUT 35 STUFFED SHELLS; SERVES 8

 INGREDIENTS

One 12-ounce box jumbo pasta shells

2 tablespoons olive oil

1 pound fresh spinach

1¼ cups shredded mozzarella cheese

3 cups ricotta cheese

2 large eggs, lightly beaten

2 cloves garlic, minced

1 cup freshly grated Parmesan cheese

⅛ teaspoon ground nutmeg

½ teaspoon kosher salt

¼ teaspoon white pepper

Marinara Sauce (recipe on next page)

¼ cup minced fresh flat-leaf parsley

I first tried these stuffed shells at a tiny Italian restaurant called Buona Gente in Long Beach, CA. They were so tasty and such a treat, I had to learn how to make them myself.

1. Preheat the oven to 350°F.

2. In a large pot of salted boiling water, cook the shells for 12 to 13 minutes, or until al dente. Drain and return to the pot. Drizzle with the olive oil and stir to coat so the pasta won't stick together.

3. In a large saucepan over medium heat, combine the spinach with ¼ cup water. Simmer, covered, for 3 to 5 minutes or until spinach is throughly wilted. Drain well and squeeze the spinach to remove excess moisture. Finely chop the spinach and set aside.

4. In a large bowl, combine the mozzarella, ricotta, eggs, garlic, spinach, ½ cup of the Parmesan, the nutmeg, and the salt and pepper. Stir to blend. Using a tablespoon, generously stuff the pasta shells with the cheese mixture. Place the stuffed shells in two 9-by-13-inch baking dishes and cover with the marinara sauce. Sprinkle evenly with the remaining ½ cup Parmesan and the parsley.

5. Bake for 25 to 30 minutes, or until the cheese is melted and the sauce looks hot and bubbly. Let cool for 5 to 10 minutes before serving.

Twist It Up

This dish is one of my all-time favorites. To twist it up, add some ground turkey or beef to the marinara sauce to make it a rich Bolognese.

MARINARA SAUCE

MAKES ABOUT 6 CUPS

INGREDIENTS

2 tablespoons olive oil

1/2 yellow onion, chopped

3 cloves garlic, minced

One 14 1/2-ounce can diced tomatoes

Two 14 1/2-ounce cans tomato sauce

2 beef bouillon cubes

1/2 teaspoon dried basil

1/2 teaspoon dried oregano

1 tablespoon chopped fresh flat-leaf parsley

2 teaspoons sugar

Kosher salt and freshly ground pepper

In a large, heavy saucepan, heat the olive oil over medium heat. Add the onion and sauté until translucent. Add the garlic and sauté for 1 minute. Add the tomatoes, tomato sauce, bouillon cubes, basil, oregano, parsley, and sugar. Stir well. Simmer and cook over low heat for 30 minutes, stirring occasionally. Season with salt and pepper to taste.

JACK'S SHEPHERD'S PIE & ROASTED GARLIC MASHED POTATOES

 SERVES 4

 INGREDIENTS

½ cup all-purpose flour

½ teaspoon salt, plus more as needed

½ teaspoon freshly ground pepper, plus more as needed

One 1¼-pound beef rib eye roast, cut into 1-inch cubes

1 tablespoon olive oil

½ cup chopped yellow onion

½ cup chopped carrot

3 cloves garlic, minced

¾ cup beef broth

½ cup chopped tomatoes (drained if canned)

2 teaspoons sugar

½ teaspoon dried thyme

½ cup frozen peas

(continued)

I came up with this recipe when I was asked to be on *The Tonight Show* with Jay Leno. Jay doesn't like vegetables very much—in fact, he's strictly a meat and potatoes guy. There *are* some vegetables in shepherd's pie, but I thought he could just eat around them. While we were taping the show, Jay tried to get me to leave them out, but I just said, "Eat them anyway!"

1. In a pie pan, combine the flour, salt, and pepper; stir well with a whisk to blend. Roll the meat in the seasoned flour to coat on all sides.

2. In a large, heavy saucepan, heat the olive oil over medium-high heat. Add the onion and carrot and sauté until tender, about 5 minutes. Add the meat to the saucepan and cook until browned on all sides, about 4 minutes. Add the garlic and sauté for 1 minute. Add the broth, tomatoes, sugar, and thyme. Stir well. Bring to a boil and reduce the heat to a simmer. Cover and cook for 25 to 30 minutes, until the carrots are just tender and the gravy is bubbly. Stir in the peas, then salt and pepper to taste.

3. Meanwhile, preheat the oven to 375°F and make the potatoes: Put the potatoes in a large pot of salted cold water, bring to a boil, and cook until tender, 15 to 20 minutes. Drain well and return to the pot. Cook, shaking the pan, over medium heat for a minute or two to cook off the excess water. Add the butter and mash the potatoes with a potato masher. Using an electric mixer on low speed, gradually beat in the milk and roasted garlic until smooth and fluffy.

continued >>>>>

 GARLIC MASHED
POTATOES

3 large baking (russet) potatoes,
peeled and diced

4 tablespoons unsalted butter
at room temperature

1/2 cup milk at room temperature

3 cloves Roasted Garlic
(recipe at right)

Twist It Up

This is a hearty dinner that doesn't take that long to make but is really satisfying and has lots of flavor. It has meat, vegetables, potatoes, and gravy all in one spoonful. If you want to twist up this recipe, just add more veggies, like zucchini or squash. You could try using different cuts of meat, like lamb or ground beef, too. The garlic mashed potatoes make a great side dish for any kind of meat or poultry. This recipe makes enough mashed potatoes for 4 side-dish servings.

4. Scoop the meat mixture into a 9 1/2-inch deep-dish pie plate or baking dish. Dollop the mashed potatoes on top and smooth with a rubber spatula.

5. Bake for 15 minutes. Set the oven to broil and cook 4 inches from the heat source for 4 to 5 minutes to brown the top. Let cool for 5 minutes before serving.

ROASTED GARLIC

Cut the top one-third off a garlic bulb. Place the bulb on a square of aluminum foil and drizzle with 1 teaspoon olive oil, then sprinkle with kosher salt and freshly ground pepper. Wrap the garlic in the aluminum foil, place on a baking sheet, and roast in a preheated 450°F oven for 35 to 40 minutes. Unwrap the foil from the garlic and let cool to the touch. The top of the garlic bulb should be a golden brown color and should feel soft but not mushy. Just squeeze the bulb to pop out the cloves.

TASTY TURKEY MEATBALLS
WITH JACK'S SPECIAL DIPPING SAUCE

 SERVES 6 TO 8

 MEATBALLS

2 1/2 pounds ground turkey

1/2 cup chopped green onions

1/2 cup chopped fresh
flat-leaf parsley

2 cloves garlic, minced

1 large egg, lightly beaten

1/2 teaspoon freshly ground
black pepper

1/4 teaspoon freshly ground
white pepper

1/2 teaspoon dried oregano

1 teaspoon dried thyme

1/2 teaspoon ground nutmeg

2 teaspoons garlic powder

4 teaspoons seasoned salt
such as Lawry's

1 teaspoon sugar

3 tablespoons all-purpose flour

2 slices stale or lightly toasted
bread, torn into 1/2-inch pieces

1/4 cup chopped tomatoes

(continued)

These meatballs are so well seasoned and yummy. You can make them nice and small and serve them as appetizers with my dipping sauce. My mom's friend Vera was the inspiration for this recipe. I tried to make these like her meatballs—moist and packed full of flavor.

1. For the meatballs: In a large bowl, combine all of the ingredients. You can use a wooden spoon to stir everything together, but to thoroughly blend the ingredients, you will need to use your spotlessly clean hands (this is very messy and fun!).

2. Shape the meatball mixture into 1 1/2- to 2-inch balls and place on a sheet of waxed paper. Spray a large skillet with nonstick cooking spray and heat over medium-high heat. Put the meatballs in the pan and brown on all sides, 3 to 4 minutes, turning

them as needed. Reduce the heat to low and cook for 20 minutes to cook through, turning occasionally.

3. Meanwhile, make the dipping sauce: In a medium saucepan, combine all of the ingredients and stir well to blend. Bring to a simmer over medium-low heat and cook for 5 minutes. Set aside and keep warm.

4. Using a slotted spoon, divide the meatballs among the serving plates. Serve with the dipping sauce alongside.

continued >>>>>

DIPPING SAUCE

¹⁄₂ cup chili sauce

¹⁄₂ cup barbecue sauce

1 cup ketchup

Twist It Up

Twist up the flavor of these meatballs by changing just a few ingredients: To give them an Italian flair, add some chopped fresh basil and freshly grated Parmesan cheese. For a Mexican touch, add ground cumin and minced fresh chile or a dash of cayenne pepper. These meatballs are great for snacks. Mom freezes the leftovers so we can microwave them for a quick fix. You can make them in sandwiches and spread the dipping sauce right on the bread. They taste great with mustard and mayo, too.

FINGER-LICKIN' GOOD BABY BACK RIBS
WITH JACK'S HOMEMADE BARBECUE SAUCE

 SERVES 4

 INGREDIENTS

3 to 4 pounds pork baby back ribs

1 lemon, scrubbed and thinly sliced

1 yellow onion, thinly sliced

 BARBECUE SAUCE

1 cup ketchup

¼ cup firmly packed brown sugar

¼ cup plus 2 tablespoons light agave nectar

¼ cup orange juice

1 teaspoon minced fresh basil

1 tablespoon minced fresh chives

6 cloves garlic, crushed

¼ teaspoon cayenne pepper

½ teaspoon sweet Hungarian paprika

2 tablespoons Worcestershire sauce

1 tablespoon Tiger Sauce or other hot sauce

½ cup chili sauce

½ teaspoon kosher salt

Baby back ribs are one of my absolute favorite foods. I made this barbecue sauce with my friend chef Chris Logan when we cooked at a charity event together in the summer of 2010. We put it on grilled chicken, but it tastes really good on my ribs, too. In fact, you can use it on just about any kind of meat you want to grill.

1. Preheat the oven to 350°F.

2. Trim and discard the excess fat from the ribs, then arrange them in a single layer in a large roasting pan. Pour in 1 cup water. Distribute the lemon and onion slices evenly over the meat. Cover with aluminum foil and bake for 1 to 1½ hours, or until the meat is just tender but not falling off the bone.

3. Meanwhile, make the barbecue sauce: In a small, heavy saucepan, combine all the ingredients and stir to blend. Bring to a simmer over low heat and cook, stirring frequently, until slightly thickened. Cook for at least 1 hour to fully develop the flavors.

4. About 30 minutes before the ribs are done, prepare a hot fire in a charcoal grill or preheat a gas grill to high. (You will definitely need a parent's help with this!)

5. Remove the ribs from the oven and let them cool to the touch. Cut the ribs into serving-size pieces (4 to 6 ribs) and place them on a platter. Using tongs, grill the ribs for 2 to 3 minutes on each side or until you get a light char on each side. Brush with the barbecue sauce and grill for 2 to 3 minutes on each side or until desired char is achieved. Remove from the grill and brush with more sauce if desired. Serve with individual bowls of sauce for dipping.

Twist It Up

Precooking my ribs before they go on the grill is the secret to making them super-moist and tender.

BEST-EVER SPINACH LASAGNA

  SERVES 8

INGREDIENTS

One 8-ounce box lasagna noodles

2 tablespoons olive oil, plus more for drizzling

½ yellow onion, chopped

4 cloves garlic, minced

1 pound ground turkey

Kosher salt and freshly ground pepper

6 cups Marinara Sauce (page 88)

2½ cups ricotta cheese

4½ cups shredded mozzarella cheese

¾ cup freshly grated Parmesan cheese

2 large eggs, lightly beaten

One 10-ounce package chopped frozen spinach, thawed, drained, and squeezed by handfuls to get rid of any excess moisture

Twist It Up

For even more flavor, add ground sausage or sautéed mushrooms to the sauce.

You won't ever need another lasagna recipe after you try this one. It's rich and creamy and cheesy and absolutely delicious. Make enough so you can have leftovers. It tastes even better the next day.

1. Preheat the oven to 375°F.

2. In a large pot of salted boiling water, cook the noodles for 7 to 8 minutes, or until almost al dente. Drain, then return to the pan and lightly drizzle with olive oil so the noodles do not stick together; toss carefully to coat. Cover loosely and set aside.

3. In a large, heavy saucepan, heat the 2 tablespoons olive oil over medium heat. Add the onion and sauté until translucent, about 3 minutes. Add the garlic and sauté for 1 minute. Add the ground turkey and cook, stirring to break up the meat, until browned. Add salt and pepper to taste. Add 4½ cups of the marinara sauce and simmer for 10 minutes.

4. In a large bowl, combine the ricotta, 3½ cups of the mozzarella, ½ cup of the Parmesan, the eggs, and the spinach. Stir until well blended.

5. Spray a 9-by-13-inch baking dish with nonstick cooking spray. Spread ¾ cup of the meat sauce evenly over the bottom of the baking dish. Place a layer of lasagna noodles over the sauce, slightly overlapping them. Spread half of the cheese mixture over the noodles and then spread with half of the remaining meat sauce. Repeat with another layer of noodles, then the remaining cheese mixture and remaining meat sauce. Top with the remaining noodles and the remaining 1½ cups marinara sauce. Sprinkle with the remaining mozzarella and Parmesan. Cover with aluminum foil and bake for 30 minutes. Remove the foil and bake for 10 minutes longer to melt the cheese and brown slightly. Let stand for 10 minutes before cutting into squares to serve.

JACK'S BAKED ZITI

 SERVES 4 TO 6

 INGREDIENTS

1 pound ziti pasta

4 tablespoons olive oil

½ yellow onion, finely chopped

4 cloves garlic, minced

3 ounces pancetta, cut into small cubes

¾ pound ground turkey

One 14½-ounce can tomato sauce

2 cups chopped tomatoes (drained if canned)

½ teaspoon dried basil

2 tablespoons chopped fresh flat-leaf parsley

2 teaspoons sugar

¼ teaspoon red pepper flakes

1 beef bouillon cube

1 teaspoon kosher salt

½ cup ricotta cheese

2 cups shredded mozzarella cheese

¾ cup freshly grated Parmesan cheese

This dish is cheesy, gooey, and a little chewy on top—it's the best! I get hungry just thinking about it. When you cook this up, no one will be able to resist it.

1. In a large pot of salted boiling water, cook the ziti for 8 to 9 minutes, or until al dente. Drain and return to the pot. Drizzle with 1 tablespoon of the olive oil and toss so the pasta does not stick together. Loosely cover and set aside.

2. Preheat the oven to 375°F.

3. In a large, heavy saucepan, heat the remaining 3 tablespoons olive oil over medium heat. Add the onion and sauté for 3 minutes, or until translucent. Add the garlic and sauté for 1 minute. Add the pancetta and cook for 3 to 4 minutes, till it just begins to get crisp. Add the ground turkey and cook, breaking it up with a spoon, for 6 to 7 minutes, or until browned. Add the tomato sauce, chopped tomatoes, basil, parsley, sugar, red pepper flakes, bouillon cube, and salt and simmer for 15 minutes, stirring occasionally. Add the ricotta and 1 cup of the mozzarella and stir well to combine.

4. Stir the sauce into the pasta to coat well. Pour into a greased 9-by-13-inch baking dish and smooth the top. Sprinkle evenly with the remaining 1 cup mozzarella and all of the Parmesan. Bake for 20 to 25 minutes, or until the cheese is melted and beginning to brown in spots.

Twist It Up

This dish does not stick around long. My brother could barely come up for air when he started eating it! It's perfect with a green salad on the side.

CHICKEN CACCIATORE

 SERVES 4 TO 6

 INGREDIENTS

3 tablespoons olive oil

Kosher salt and freshly ground pepper

One frying chicken, about 3½ pounds, cut into serving pieces

1 yellow onion, chopped

4 cloves garlic, minced

2 green bell peppers, seeded, deveined, and chopped

8 ounces cremini mushrooms, sliced

Two 14½-ounce cans chopped tomatoes

Two 14½-ounce cans tomato sauce

1 cup chicken broth

2 teaspoons brown sugar

½ teaspoon dried oregano

¼ teaspoon dried thyme

3 tablespoons chopped fresh flat-leaf parsley

1 pound linguine pasta

Freshly grated Parmesan cheese for serving

This is a classic Italian chicken dish with a rich tomato-based sauce. The peppers, onion, and mushrooms, paired with all the herbs, are amazing. It is a simple and easy dinner to prepare—and I never get tired of eating it.

1. In a large, heavy pot, warm the olive oil over medium-high heat. Generously salt and pepper the chicken pieces, add to the pot, and brown on all sides. Using tongs, transfer to a plate and set aside.

2. Add the onion, garlic, green peppers, and mushrooms to the pot, then reduce the heat to medium and cook for 5 minutes, or until the onion is soft. Add the tomatoes, tomato sauce, broth, brown sugar, oregano, thyme, and parsley and stir well. Return the browned chicken to the pot. Bring to a boil and reduce the heat to a simmer. Cover and cook, stirring occasionally, for 1 to 1½ hours, or until the chicken is cooked through and tender.

3. When the chicken and sauce are almost done, cook the linguine in a large pot of salted boiling water for about 9 minutes, or until al dente. Drain. Divide the pasta among the plates and spoon the chicken and its sauce next to the pasta. Serve with the fresh Parmesan alongside for sprinkling.

Twist It Up

To make the sauce richer, add ¾ cup heavy cream or half-and-half while the chicken is simmering. Stir to be sure the mixture is well combined. This dish is terrific with pasta, but it's really good with garlic mashed potatoes (page 91), too. If you go the potato route, be sure to have some fresh green beans on the side.

JACK'S SPAGHETTI ALLA CARBONARA

  SERVES 4 TO 6

INGREDIENTS

2 large eggs at room temperature

1 cup freshly grated Parmesan cheese

$2/3$ cup half-and-half, warmed

1 pound spaghetti pasta

3 tablespoons extra-virgin olive oil

8 ounces pancetta, cut into small cubes

$1/2$ cup finely chopped yellow onion

2 cloves garlic, minced

Kosher salt and freshly ground pepper

$1/2$ cup chopped fresh flat-leaf parsley (optional)

This pasta is light and perfect for brunch or a leisurely lunch. It is yummy and satisfying but so different from the pastas I normally make. I feel really Italian when I eat this dish.

1. Break the eggs into a medium bowl and add $1/2$ cup of the cheese and all of the half-and-half. Whisk to blend well.

2. In a large pot of salted boiling water, cook the spaghetti for 7 to 9 minutes, or until al dente.

3. While the pasta is cooking, heat the olive oil in a large sauté pan over medium heat. Add the pancetta and sauté until it just starts to become crisp, about 4 minutes. Add the onion and sauté for 3 minutes, or until translucent. Add the garlic and sauté for 1 minute.

4. Drain the hot pasta and add to the sauté pan with the pancetta, onion, garlic, and all the pan juices. Stir in the egg mixture to coat the pasta evenly. Season with salt to taste and generously season with pepper. If desired, add the parsley and toss again. Serve immediately with the remaining Parmesan alongside for sprinkling.

Twist It Up

Pancetta gives this dish its delicious flavor. In a pinch, I've made it with bacon, and I have to say, although it's not as authentic, it tastes pretty good that way, too.

APPETIZERS & SIDE DISHES

Sometimes, people forget just how important appetizers and side dishes are to a meal. The right sides can transform an average meal into a sensational experience. For me, side dishes are like skateboarding: I love it, but school and organized sports come first, so I just squeeze in skateboarding whenever I can. Someday, I'd like to skateboard all day and then just make a bunch of side dishes for dinner!

JACK'S STUFFED MUSHROOMS

 MAKES ABOUT 35 STUFFED MUSHROOMS; SERVES 10 AS AN APPETIZER

 INGREDIENTS

1 pound cremini mushrooms

2 tablespoons unsalted butter

2 tablespoons olive oil

1 large shallot, minced

7 cloves garlic, minced

¾ cup freshly grated Parmesan cheese, plus 1 tablespoon for garnish

¾ cup shredded mozzarella cheese

¼ cup dried bread crumbs

¼ cup minced fresh flat-leaf parsley, plus 1 tablespoon for garnish

¼ teaspoon kosher salt

You won't be able to resist these stuffed mushrooms. I made them for both of my Cooking Up Dreams fund-raising events, and each bite is a morsel of cheesy, garlicky, herby bread crumbs in a baked mushroom cap. This might be my all-time favorite appetizer.

1. Preheat the oven to 375°F.

2. Remove the stems from the mushrooms, set the caps aside, and finely chop the stems. In a large skillet, melt the butter with the olive oil over medium heat. Add the shallot, chopped mushroom stems, and garlic and sauté until tender, about 5 minutes.

3. In a large bowl, combine the ¾ cup Parmesan, mozzarella, bread crumbs, ¼ cup parsley, salt, and cooked mushroom mixture. Stir well with a fork. Using your hands or a small spoon, put about 1 tablespoon of the mixture into each mushroom cap. Place the stuffed mushroom caps on an ungreased baking sheet and bake for about 20 minutes, or until the cheese has melted and the filling is lightly browned. Sprinkle on the remaining Parmesan cheese and parsley. Serve warm.

Twist It UP

The best thing about making stuffed mushrooms is that you can add your favorite flavors to the mix. Try using ⅓ cup minced fresh spinach instead of the parsley and subbing feta for the Parmesan cheese.

CAESAR SALAD CUPS

MAKES 24 SALAD CUPS; SERVES 10 TO 12 AS AN APPETIZER OR SIDE DISH

INGREDIENTS

24 slices white bread

7 tablespoons unsalted butter at room temperature

1 tablespoon garlic powder

4 cups finely chopped romaine lettuce

½ cup Caesar salad dressing

¾ cup freshly grated Parmesan cheese

Caesar salad is a classic, and I just love eating it in these cups. My mom made them once and I liked them so much, I kind of stole her idea. (I know she doesn't mind.) Not only do they taste good, they look amazing, too.

1. Preheat the oven to 350°F.

2. Place 2 to 3 slices of bread on a cutting board, then use a rolling pin to flatten the bread to the thickness of a thin pancake. Using a drinking glass as a cookie cutter, cut a round out of each piece of bread. Repeat for all 24 slices of bread. Push the rounds into 24 ungreased mini muffin cups.

3. Put the butter in a microwave-safe bowl and melt in the microwave on high, 10 to 15 seconds. Using a pastry brush, coat the bread with butter and sprinkle with garlic powder. Bake until lightly browned, 6 to 8 minutes.

4. Meanwhile, put the lettuce in a medium bowl and pour in the Caesar dressing, tossing well with salad tongs. Place the toasted bread cups on a large platter and fill each with 2 to 3 tablespoons of salad. Sprinkle with the Parmesan cheese and serve.

Twist It Up

Each of these bite-size morsels is like eating a perfect bite of garlic bread and Caesar salad at the same time. You can actually fill these mini bread cups with any kind of salad you like, such as a mix of tomato, basil, and mozzarella—just remember to cut up the vegetables really small so they fit into the little cups.

QUICK SMASHED
BABY RED POTATOES & CHIVES

 SERVES 4

 INGREDIENTS

8 small red potatoes

6 tablespoons (¾ stick) unsalted butter at room temperature

⅓ cup sour cream at room temperature

⅓ cup milk at room temperature

½ cup chopped fresh chives

½ teaspoon garlic powder

Kosher salt and freshly ground pepper

These potatoes are easy and fast to make, so you'll never have an excuse not to make smashed potatoes again. The secret ingredient is the potato skins! That's right: Leave some on the potatoes to give this dish great color, texture, and flavor.

1. Puncture the potatoes with a fork and place on a microwave-safe plate. Microwave on high for about 10 minutes, or until fork-tender, turning the potatoes halfway through (**caution:** microwave times may vary).

2. With a vegetable peeler, peel away half of each potato's skin. In a large saucepan, melt the butter over low heat. Add the potatoes. Using a potato masher, mash together the potatoes and butter just until the butter is mixed into the potatoes. Add the sour cream and milk and mash until just smashed, or coarsely mashed.

3. Stir in the chives and garlic powder and generously season with salt and pepper. Serve immediately.

Twist It UP

If you have time to roast garlic for this dish (page 91), it will give your smashed potatoes a nutty and deliciously smooth garlic flavor. Just replace the garlic powder with 2 tablespoons roasted garlic cloves.

AWESOME ARTICHOKES

 SERVES 4 AS A SIDE DISH OR APPETIZER

 INGREDIENTS

2 large artichokes

5 bay leaves

1 1/2 tablespoons olive oil

1 1/2 tablespoons chopped fresh basil

1 large lemon, cut into quarters

 LEMON MAYONNAISE

3/4 cup mayonnaise

Juice from 1/2 large lemon

3/4 teaspoon ground dried oregano

I think the secret to these artichokes is the oil and lemon in the water, which adds great flavor and moistness to this unique veggie.

1. Trim off the top fourth of the artichokes, then cut the bottom stems even with the base. Put the artichokes in a large pot and add enough water to cover completely. Add the bay leaves, olive oil, basil, and lemon wedges to the pot.

2. Cover the pot and bring to a boil. Reduce the heat to medium and cook, uncovered, for 45 minutes, or until the artichokes are tender and the leaves can be pulled off easily.

3. Using tongs, transfer the artichokes to a large bowl and let cool slightly.

4. For the lemon mayonnaise: In a small bowl, stir together the mayonnaise and lemon juice. Generously sprinkle with the oregano.

5. Slice each artichoke in half lengthwise. Serve each artichoke half on a salad plate, with the lemon mayonnaise alongside for dipping.

Twist It Up

The artichoke is one of my favorite vegetables. It tastes a little bit like an avocado but it definitely has a unique flavor all its own. I like scraping the meat off the base of each leaf with my teeth, but the best part is the heart. You have to dig out the prickly choke with a teaspoon and discard it before you reach the heart, but it tastes great getting there! The lemon mayonnaise dip is delicious with the artichoke. The ground oregano is the surprise secret ingredient.

SUPER STEAMED VEGGIES

 SERVES 4

 INGREDIENTS

3 vegetable bouillon cubes

4 cups bite-size cut fresh vegetables, like broccoli, peas, carrots, zucchini, and/or green beans

1/2 teaspoon seasoned salt such as Lawry's

1/2 teaspoon Old Bay Seasoning

1/4 teaspoon freshly ground black pepper or red pepper flakes

2 tablespoons fresh lemon juice

Lemon wedges or ranch dressing for serving (optional)

True story: I actually like vegetables more than dessert! I've always been that way. Steaming veggies is one of my favorite ways to cook them up—now I hope it will be one of yours, too.

1. Put a steaming rack in the bottom of a large pot. Fill the pot with water to the bottom of the steamer basket. Put the bouillon cubes in the water.

2. Put the veggies in the steamer basket and add the seasoned salt, Old Bay, pepper, and lemon juice.

3. Cover the pot and place over medium-high heat. Cook for 15 to 20 minutes, or until the veggies are crisp-tender. Remove the lid and use tongs to transfer the veggies to a bowl or plates. Serve immediately with lemon wedges or ranch dressing, if desired.

Twist It Up

The vegetable bouillon is one of this dish's secret ingredients. By adding it to the water, the veggies are infused with an extra boost of flavor. When it's time to serve the veggies, I like to squeeze a little more lemon juice on them or have some ranch dressing on the side.

PICNIC-STYLE BAKED BEANS

  SERVES 8

INGREDIENTS

1 pound sliced bacon

Two 28-ounce cans baked beans

$\frac{1}{4}$ cup barbecue sauce

$\frac{1}{4}$ cup ketchup

1 tablespoon dry mustard

$\frac{1}{4}$ cup packed brown sugar

1 tablespoon molasses

$\frac{1}{4}$ cup distilled white vinegar

These beans may not be made from scratch, but they taste totally homemade. I know they do, because I brought them to a potluck party where there were other bean dishes. We had a "bean-off"— and my beans won! I guarantee that if you bring these to a "bean-off," yours will win, too.

1. In a large skillet, cook the bacon over medium heat until it is crisp but still chewy. Using a slotted metal spatula, transfer to paper towels to drain.

2. Pour the beans into a large, heavy saucepan and heat over medium heat for about 5 minutes. Using your hands, crumble the bacon into the beans. Stir in the barbecue sauce, ketchup, mustard, brown sugar, molasses, and vinegar. Simmer for 45 minutes, stirring occasionally. Taste and adjust the seasoning. Serve hot.

Twist It Up

It may sound strange, but beans can taste great when they're sweet. Just add a little more brown sugar or molasses if you want to sweeten this recipe up. For more zing, just add more vinegar.

WARM RED POTATO & CORN SALAD

 SERVES 8

 INGREDIENTS

2½ pounds small red potatoes

One 16-ounce bag frozen white corn kernels, thawed

1 pound sliced bacon

1 red onion, finely chopped

1 red bell pepper, seeded, deveined, and finely chopped

¼ teaspoon red pepper flakes

2 teaspoons sugar

¼ cup rice vinegar

⅓ cup chicken broth

1 teaspoon kosher salt, plus more to taste

¾ cup chopped fresh flat-leaf parsley

Freshly ground pepper

This potato salad is sweet and savory, but also warm and chewy, with that wonderful bacon mixed in. I can eat this all by itself, but it tastes even better when you serve some of my fried chicken or baby back ribs with it.

1. Put the potatoes in a large pot of salted cold water. Cover and bring to a boil. Cook for 15 to 18 minutes, or until the potatoes are firm but fork-tender and the skins are still intact. Add the corn and cook for 3 minutes. Drain the vegetables and rinse with cold water to stop cooking. Cut the potatoes into quarters and place in a bowl with the corn.

2. In a large skillet, cook the bacon over medium heat until crisp but still chewy. Using a slotted metal spatula, transfer to paper towels to drain. Crumble the bacon into the bowl with the potatoes. Add the onion to the bacon fat in the pan and cook for 5 minutes. Add the bell pepper, red pepper flakes, sugar, vinegar, and chicken broth and bring to a boil. Reduce the heat to a simmer and add the salt and parsley. Pour over the potato mixture and toss to combine. Season with salt and pepper to taste. Serve warm.

Twist It Up

If you want to give this recipe some Italian flair, add ¾ cup chopped tomatoes instead of the bell pepper, then add 3 tablespoons chopped fresh basil and ⅓ cup freshly grated Parmesan cheese.

ROASTED SWEET POTATO WEDGES

  SERVES 4

INGREDIENTS

½ cup olive oil

2 cups dried bread crumbs

1 teaspoon onion powder

1 teaspoon garlic powder

½ teaspoon kosher salt

½ teaspoon freshly ground pepper

1 teaspoon sweet Hungarian paprika

3 sweet potatoes, cut into ½-inch-thick wedges

These potatoes are a total crowd-pleaser. They're so sweet and crunchy that no one can stop eating them. Plus, they're super easy to make.

1. Preheat the oven to 425°F. Spray a roasting pan with nonstick cooking spray.

2. Pour the olive oil into a medium bowl. In a 9½-inch pie pan or shallow bowl, combine the bread crumbs, onion powder, garlic powder, salt, pepper, and paprika.

3. Dip each potato wedge into the olive oil to coat on both sides, shake off the excess oil, then dredge in the bread crumb mixture to coat evenly.

Place on the prepared pan. Repeat with the remaining wedges. Bake for about 45 minutes, turning every 15 minutes so the potatoes will be crisp on all sides. Serve immediately.

Twist It UP

These sweet potatoes taste amazing drizzled with Creamy Pesto Sauce (page 70). You can also dip these wedges into ketchup or my tangy homemade barbecue sauce (page 96).

SWEETS

I guess I'm a bit different from lots of kids—I tend to prefer desserts that are a little more savory than sweet. Don't get me wrong: I like a nice, big slice of chocolate cake like everyone else does, but I also really like more fruity desserts, or even desserts that have veggies in them, like carrot cake with cream cheese frosting.

Baking is a whole different way of cooking. You have to be sure to measure properly so your cakes and cookies turn out just right. (Some people even call baking a "science.") And when you bake for someone, they feel really special . . . and that always makes me feel really good, too.

BAKED APPLES

 SERVES 8

 INGREDIENTS

8 apples of your choice
(I like Fuji or Gala)

$1/2$ cup packed brown sugar

$1/2$ teaspoon ground cinnamon

$1/4$ teaspoon ground cloves

$1/2$ teaspoon ground nutmeg

4 tablespoons unsalted butter

$3/4$ cup apple juice

Whipped cream or vanilla
ice cream for serving

This dessert tastes like apple pie filling, but it's a lot quicker and easier to make. My brother and I like to make these in the winter. We eat them as a treat after we've finished our homework.

1. Preheat the oven to 350°F.

2. Core the apples and peel the top third of each one. Place the apples in an 11-by-7-inch baking pan or in a 10-inch cast-iron frying pan. In a small bowl, combine the brown sugar, cinnamon, cloves, and nutmeg. Fill the apple centers with the sugar mixture. Dot the center of each apple with $1/2$ tablespoon butter, then pour the juice evenly over the apples.

3. Bake for 50 to 60 minutes, or until the apples are fork-tender. Baste occasionally with juices from the pan. Serve warm, with whipped cream or vanilla ice cream.

Twist It up

I like to have this dessert with a big scoop of vanilla bean ice cream— it's a great pairing! For an awesome presentation, sometimes we cook the apples in a 10-inch cast-iron pan—it keeps them hot for a long time, and it looks terrific!

CHOCOLATE BROWNIES

 MAKES 24 BROWNIES

 INGREDIENTS

¾ cup semisweet chocolate chips

½ cup (1 stick) plus
2 tablespoons unsalted butter
at room temperature

2 cups sugar

4 large eggs, lightly beaten

1 cup all-purpose flour

2 tablespoons unsweetened
cocoa powder

¼ teaspoon salt

1 teaspoon vanilla extract

Powdered sugar for dusting

These brownies are rich and chocolaty, crisp on the top like a cookie, and gooey and soft in the middle like a cake. This is a one-pan dessert that no one will turn down—in fact, count on requests for seconds.

1. Preheat the oven to 350°F. Butter a 9-by-13-inch baking dish or pan.

2. Put the chocolate chips and the butter in a microwave-safe bowl and microwave on high for 45 seconds. Stir the chocolate mixture and heat for 10 to 15 seconds more if the mixture is not completely melted. Repeat if necessary until the chocolate mixture is smooth. Add the sugar, eggs, flour, cocoa powder, salt, and vanilla and stir until well blended.

3. Pour the batter into the prepared pan. Bake for 25 to 30 minutes in a glass baking dish, 30 to 35 minutes in a metal baking pan, or until a toothpick inserted 2 inches from the side of the pan comes out almost clean.

4. Let cool in the pan completely before cutting (otherwise, the brownies will fall apart). Lightly dust with powdered sugar and cut into 24 brownies to serve.

Twist It Up

To give these brownies a little more crunch, add ½ cup chopped walnuts to the batter before baking. Pair some vanilla ice cream with my brownies and you've got a perfect dessert to serve when friends come over. (Warning: These brownies are dangerously delicious and you may gain several pounds just by reading this recipe!)

BEST-EVER BIRTHDAY CUPCAKES

 MAKES 24 CUPCAKES

INGREDIENTS

2¼ cups cake flour

1¼ cups sugar

1 tablespoon baking powder

1 teaspoon salt

½ cup (1 stick) unsalted butter at room temperature

1 cup milk at room temperature

2 large eggs at room temperature

1 teaspoon vanilla extract

Chocolate Frosting (recipe follows)

Who doesn't love cupcakes? They're easy to make and fun to eat, so making them for birthday parties is a no-brainer. When I eat cupcakes, I like licking off the frosting first and saving the cake for last.

1. Preheat the oven to 375°F. Line 24 muffin cups with paper baking cups.

2. In a medium bowl, combine the flour, sugar, baking powder, and salt. Stir with a whisk to blend. Using an electric mixer on medium speed, cream the butter and milk for 2 minutes, stopping once or twice to scrape the sides and bottom of the bowl with a rubber spatula. Add the flour mixture and beat until blended. Add the eggs and vanilla and beat for 2 minutes more. Spoon the batter into the lined muffin cups, filling them three-fourths full.

3. Bake for 18 to 20 minutes, or until a toothpick inserted into a cupcake comes out clean. Immediately remove the cupcakes from the pan and let cool completely on wire racks. Spread the frosting onto the cooled cupcakes. Let the frosting set for about 30 minutes.

Twist It Up

I like to pair these little moist cakes with my creamy chocolate frosting, but you could use almost any frosting, including the Yummy Chocolate Frosting on page 140.

CHOCOLATE FROSTING

  **MAKES ENOUGH FOR
24 CUPCAKES**

INGREDIENTS

4 ounces unsweetened baking
chocolate, chopped

½ cup (1 stick) unsalted butter
at room temperature

One 1-pound box powdered sugar

4 to 6 tablespoons half-and-half

1 tablespoon vanilla extract

This dark chocolate frosting is perfect on the Best-Ever Birthday
Cupcakes. There's nothing like the classic pairing of sweet chocolate frosting and yellow cake.

1. Put the chocolate in a microwave-
safe bowl and microwave on high for
20 seconds and stir. If the mixture is
not smooth, repeat until the chocolate is completely melted. Let cool
for 1 or 2 minutes.

2. Using an electric mixer on
low speed, beat together the butter,
sugar, 4 tablespoons half-and-half,
and the vanilla until smooth. Add
the cooled melted chocolate and
stir until well blended. If the frosting is too thick, beat in more half-
and-half, a few drops at a time.
If the frosting becomes too thin,
beat in a small amount of powdered sugar.

Twist It Up

You know how I feel about yellow
cake cupcakes, but this dark chocolate frosting can be used to top
many different cakes. Try it on my
chocolate birthday cake recipe (page
139)—it tastes great on that, too.

CARROT CAKE

 MAKES ONE 9-BY-13-INCH CAKE

 INGREDIENTS

2 cups all-purpose flour

2 teaspoons baking powder

1 teaspoon baking soda

¾ teaspoon salt

2 teaspoons ground cinnamon

½ teaspoon ground nutmeg

½ teaspoon ground cloves

1 cup granulated sugar

1¼ cups packed light brown sugar

1 cup canola oil

½ cup (1 stick) unsalted butter
at room temperature

¼ cup milk

4 large eggs at room temperature

1 tablespoon vanilla extract

3 cups lightly packed shredded
peeled carrots

Cream Cheese Frosting
(recipe follows)

This cake is sweet and savory, moist, and just plain yummy—
my kind of dessert.

1. Preheat the oven to 350°F. Grease and flour the bottom and sides of a 9-by-13-inch baking pan. Knock out the excess flour.

2. In a medium bowl, combine the flour, baking powder, baking soda, salt, and spices. Stir with a whisk to blend. Using an electric mixer on low speed, beat together the white and brown sugars, oil, and butter and whisk until smooth. Add the milk, eggs, and vanilla and beat for about 1 minute, or until well blended. Gradually add the flour mixture and beat on low for 1 to 2 minutes or until combined. Stir in the carrots until blended. Pour the batter into the prepared pan and smooth the top.

3. Bake for 40 to 45 minutes, or until a toothpick inserted into the center comes out clean. Transfer the pan to a wire rack and let the cake cool completely, about 1 hour. Spread the frosting evenly over the cake and let set for 30 minutes before cutting into squares.

Twist It Up

Twist this up and turn it into an apple cake by substituting 3 cups chopped cored and peeled apples for the shredded carrots. Or make it into a zucchini cake by using 3 cups shredded zucchini instead of the carrots.

CREAM CHEESE FROSTING

**MAKES ENOUGH FOR
ONE 9-BY-13-INCH CAKE**

 INGREDIENTS

One 8-ounce package cream cheese
at room temperature

4 tablespoons unsalted butter
at room temperature

2 to 3 teaspoons milk

1 teaspoon vanilla extract

3½ cups sifted powdered sugar

This frosting is so simple—just cream cheese sweetened with sugar, and then made even creamier by adding a little butter. It's easy and fast to make and a great topping for the carrot cake.

1. Using an electric mixer on low speed, blend together the cream cheese, butter, milk, and vanilla until smooth.

2. Gradually beat in the powdered sugar, ½ cup at a time, until smooth and spreadable. If the frosting gets too thick, beat in more milk, a few drops at a time. If the frosting becomes too thin, beat in a small amount of powdered sugar.

Twist It Up

This frosting is perfect for twisting it up! Add 1 teaspoon grated orange or lemon zest for a citrusy taste. Be sure to refrigerate the frosted cake (or any extra frosting), because the cream cheese will spoil if it's left out at room temperature.

OLD-FASHIONED APPLE PIE

  SERVES 8

INGREDIENTS

3½ pounds Gravenstein, Pippin, or Granny Smith apples, peeled, cored, and thinly sliced (about 8 cups)

1 tablespoon fresh lemon juice

1 cup packed light brown sugar

¼ cup all-purpose flour

1½ teaspoons ground cinnamon

¼ teaspoon ground ginger

1 package (two 9-inch rounds) store-bought piecrust at room temperature

2 tablespoons unsalted butter

2 teaspoons water

1 tablespoon granulated sugar

Maple Syrup Whipped Cream (recipe follows)

This dessert always makes me think of home and being with my family. Apple pie is just one of those comforting foods with amazing powers.

1. Preheat the oven to 425°F and position a rack on the middle shelf of the oven.

2. In a large bowl, combine the apples, lemon juice, brown sugar, flour, cinnamon, and ginger. Stir to blend well, then set aside.

3. Unroll the piecrusts and place one in a 9-inch glass pie plate. Press the crust firmly against the sides and bottom, then trim the bottom crust even with the edge of the pie plate. Pour in the apple filling and dot the top with the butter. Lay the second crust on top of the mixture. Trim the top crust to a 1-inch overhang and fold the edges under the edges of the bottom crust. Using your forefingers and thumbs, crimp the crust to make a scalloped edge.

Brush the top lightly with the water and sprinkle with the granulated sugar. With a small knife, cut 4 slits in the center of the top crust in a circular pattern. To prevent the rim from browning, wrap it with a 2- to 3-inch-wide strip of aluminum foil.

4. Place the pie on a rimmed baking sheet on the middle rack of the oven. Bake for 30 minutes. Remove the foil and bake for 20 to 30 minutes longer, or until the apples are fork-tender. Let cool on a rack. This pie is best served warm with Maple Syrup Whipped Cream (page 134).

Twist It Up

For a treat that's hard to beat, top off this warm pie with some vanilla ice cream. The only thing that makes it taste better is having friends and family to share it with.

MAPLE SYRUP WHIPPED CREAM

  MAKES 3 CUPS

INGREDIENTS

1½ cups heavy cream, chilled

3 tablespoons maple syrup

1 teaspoon vanilla extract

I made this whipped cream for my very first Cooking Up Dreams event when I was seven. My friend chef Steve Mathews showed me how to make it. We paired it with pumpkin pie, but it's good with apple pie, too.

1. In a metal bowl (preferably chilled, because cream whips better and faster when it's really cold), combine the cream, maple syrup, and vanilla. Using an electric mixer on low speed, beat the cream for 1 or 2 minutes until it gets nice and bubbly, then increase the speed to high. Beat until soft peaks form, 3 or 4 minutes more.

2. Use the whipped cream immediately, or cover and refrigerate for up to 2 hours. Stir before using.

Twist It Up

This whipped cream goes with just about any kind of apple or pumpkin dessert. It's so good, I like to eat it all by itself! You can also flavor it with spices like ground cinnamon or nutmeg. Just add a dash before beating.

SENSATIONAL SUGAR COOKIES

 MAKES ABOUT 3 DOZEN COOKIES

 INGREDIENTS

3 cups all-purpose flour

1 teaspoon baking powder

$\frac{1}{4}$ teaspoon salt

1 cup (2 sticks) unsalted butter at room temperature

1$\frac{1}{4}$ cups granulated sugar

1 large egg

1 tablespoon milk at room temperature

1 teaspoon vanilla extract

Powdered sugar for rolling dough

Hard Cookie Icing (recipe follows)

I made these cookies as a present to my third-grade teacher for Teacher Appreciation Week. I decorated them with icing and wrapped them up in colored cellophane. They looked amazing, I must say! This recipe makes awesome cookies for Santa, too.

1. In a medium bowl, combine the flour, baking powder, and salt. Stir with a whisk to blend. Using an electric mixer on medium speed, beat together the butter and granulated sugar until combined. Add the egg, milk, and vanilla and beat until well blended. Add the dry ingredients to the butter mixture and beat on low speed until the mixture pulls away from the side of the bowl. On a lightly floured work surface, roll the dough into a ball. Divide in half and flatten each piece into a disc. Wrap in waxed paper or plastic wrap. Refrigerate for at least 2 hours or overnight.

2. Preheat the oven to 400°F. Grease 2 baking sheets.

3. Remove one half of the dough from the refrigerator. Sprinkle a work surface with powdered sugar. Using a rolling pin, roll out the dough to $\frac{1}{8}$ to $\frac{1}{4}$ inch thick. Cut into your choice of shapes with cookie cutters. Place the cookies 1 inch apart on the prepared pans.

4. Bake for 6 to 8 minutes, or just until the cookies begin to brown on the edges. Let cool on the baking sheets for 2 minutes, then transfer the cookies to wire racks to cool completely before icing.

Twist It Up

Rolling the dough nice and thin makes these cookies crisp and crunchy. You can sprinkle colored sugar right on them, but the icing makes them look spectacular—and taste even better.

HARD COOKIE ICING

MAKES ENOUGH FOR ABOUT 3 DOZEN COOKIES

 INGREDIENTS

3 cups powdered sugar

2 tablespoons milk at room temperature

7½ teaspoons corn syrup

¾ teaspoon vanilla extract

Food colorings of choice

This icing dries hard and shiny and not only makes my sugar cookies look terrific, it will make you feel like you're a real pastry chef. Use your imagination to create little works of art. It's just like painting, so it's fun and easy to do!

1. In a medium bowl, combine the sugar and milk and stir until smooth. Add the corn syrup and vanilla and, using an electric mixer on medium speed, beat until smooth. If the icing gets too thick, add more corn syrup.

2. Divide the icing among separate bowls and add food coloring to the desired intensity. Using a pastry bag or pastry brush, paint each cookie with the icing. If you want to add colored sugar or sprinkles, wait about 1 minute for the icing to begin to dry so the colors won't run.

Twist It Up

This icing dries fast and hard, and it makes my sugar cookies taste incredible! The more color and detail you add, the more amazing your cookies will look. Layering the icing colors is the secret to turning these cookies into little master-pieces. For example, if you have a cookie that is in the shape of a bear, first use one color of icing to color in its fur. Let dry for 3 to 4 minutes, then go back with a different color or colors and add his eyes, eyebrows, nose, and mouth. To do fine detail, you will need to use a smaller pastry brush or a fine-tipped pastry bag. As long as you wait for each color to dry, you can keep going back to add as much detail as you want. I guarantee everyone will love these cookies. There's only one problem: They will look too good to eat!

JACK'S STRAWBERRY SHORTCAKE

  MAKES ONE 9-BY-5-INCH LOAF; SERVES 6

INGREDIENTS

1½ cups sifted cake flour

1 teaspoon baking powder

¼ teaspoon salt

¾ cup (1½ sticks) unsalted butter at room temperature

1½ cups sifted powdered sugar, plus more for dusting

3 large eggs at room temperature

½ teaspoon vanilla extract

½ cup milk

3 cups sliced fresh strawberries

¼ cup granulated sugar, plus more if needed

Whipped cream or vanilla ice cream for serving (optional)

I love strawberry shortcake not only because it tastes so good, but because it's a dessert that says "summer." This dessert is a slam-dunk! Everyone likes it, and I guarantee they'll always have room for it, no matter how hearty the dinner.

1. Preheat the oven to 350°F. Grease and flour a 9-by-5-inch loaf pan. Knock out the excess flour.

2. In a medium bowl, combine the flour, baking powder and salt. Stir with a whisk to blend. Using an electric mixer on medium speed, cream together the butter and powdered sugar until light and fluffy. Add the eggs, one at a time, beating well after each addition. Beat in the vanilla and milk. Turn the mixer to low and gradually beat in the flour mixture, stopping once or twice to scrape down the sides and bottom of the bowl with a rubber spatula.

3. Pour the batter into the prepared pan and smooth the top. Bake for 45 to 55 minutes, or until a toothpick inserted into the center of the cake comes out clean. Let the cake cool in the pan on a wire rack for 5 minutes, then run a knife around the edges and unmold onto the rack to cool completely.

4. In a large bowl, combine the strawberries and the granulated sugar. With a potato masher, mash some of the fruit to create a sauce. Taste and adjust the sweetness if necessary. Use now or refrigerate for up to 2 days.

5. Cut the cake into 1-inch-thick slices. Spoon about ¼ cup of the strawberry mixture over each slice and dust with powdered sugar. Top with whipped cream or vanilla ice cream if you like.

Twist It Up

You can use other fresh fruits or berries in place of the strawberries. "Berry" good alternatives include blueberries, sliced peaches, and sliced apricots.

JACK'S BEST CHOCOLATE BIRTHDAY CAKE

 MAKES ONE 2-LAYER CAKE

 INGREDIENTS

1 cup (2 sticks) unsalted butter at room temperature

2 ½ cups sugar

2 large eggs at room temperature

½ cup milk at room temperature

½ cup strong coffee at room temperature

1 teaspoon baking soda

1 teaspoon baking powder

¾ teaspoon salt

⅔ cup unsweetened cocoa powder

2 cups all-purpose flour

½ cup boiling water

1½ teaspoons vanilla extract

Yummy Chocolate Frosting (recipe follows)

Making a cake is a really *sweet* way to show someone how much you care. Bake my cake for someone special, and see how good it will make you feel.

1. Preheat the oven to 350°F. Butter and flour the bottom and sides of two 9-inch round cake pans; knock out the excess flour.

2. Using an electric mixer on medium speed, cream together the butter and sugar until light and fluffy. Add the eggs and beat until smooth.

3. In a small bowl, combine the milk, coffee, baking soda, baking powder, and salt and whisk to blend. Sift the cocoa with the flour into a medium bowl.

4. Using the electric mixer set on medium speed, alternately add the milk mixture and flour mixture to the batter in three increments, ending with the flour mixture. Scrape down the bottom and sides of the bowl with a rubber spatula. Pour in the boiling water and stir well. Add the vanilla and stir until blended.

5. Divide the batter evenly between the prepared pans and smooth the tops. Bake for 30 to 35 minutes, or until a toothpick inserted into the center of a cake comes out clean. Transfer to wire racks and let cool completely in the pans.

6. To frost the cake: Run a knife around the edges of one cake and unmold onto a large plate. Using a metal spatula, spread 1 cup frosting over the top of the cake. Unmold the second layer and place it on top of the first layer. Frost the top and sides with the remaining frosting.

Twist It UP

This chocolate cake is super-moist and rich. To twist it up a little, I like to add ¾ cup sliced strawberries or bananas between the layers with the frosting. The fruit is an added surprise when you cut into the cake.

YUMMY CHOCOLATE FROSTING

**MAKES ENOUGH FOR
ONE 2-LAYER CAKE OR
24 CUPCAKES**

 INGREDIENTS

3 cups powdered sugar

1/4 cup unsweetened cocoa powder

1/2 cup (1 stick) unsalted butter,
melted

4 to 6 tablespoons milk
at room temperature

1 teaspoon vanilla extract

This creamy milk chocolate frosting is so good with my chocolate cake recipe. It's great on cupcakes, too, like my Best-Ever
Birthday Cupcakes (page 126).

Sift together the powdered sugar
and cocoa into a medium bowl. Add
the butter, 4 tablespoons milk, and
the vanilla and blend with an electric
mixer on high speed for 4 to 5 minutes, or until smooth. If the frosting
is too thick, add 1 to 2 tablespoons
more milk.

Twist It Up

To decorate this cake and give
it added flavor, I like to sprinkle
sweetened coconut shavings, colored sprinkles, or chopped nuts
all over the top and sides.

BERRY DELICIOUS PARFAIT

 MAKES 6 PARFAITS

 INGREDIENTS

¾ cup whipped cream cheese

1¼ cups marshmallow creme

3 cups sliced fresh strawberries

1 cup fresh raspberries

1 tablespoon powdered sugar

10 graham crackers

½ cup (1 stick) unsalted butter, melted

½ cup packed brown sugar

6 fresh mint leaves for garnish

This recipe takes fruit and adds a surprise: marshmallow creme! Not only does this taste delicious, it's a feast for the eyes, too.

1. In a medium bowl, stir together the cream cheese and marshmallow creme until thoroughly blended. In another medium bowl, combine the strawberries, raspberries, and powdered sugar.

2. Put the graham crackers in a gallon-size plastic zip-top bag, push out the air, and seal the bag. Using a rolling pin, crush the crackers to make coarse crumbs. Pour the cracker crumbs into a bowl, then add the melted butter and brown sugar and stir well with a fork.

3. Set 6 serving glasses on a work surface. Scoop 1 heaping tablespoon of the graham cracker mixture into the bottom of each glass. Then spoon ¼ cup of the strawbery mixture over the crumbs. Place 1 heaping tablespoon of the mashmallow mixture over the fruit . Repeat with the remaining ingredients, ending with the marshmallow mixture. You will have 2 layers of crumbs, 2 layers of cream, and 2 layers of fruit in each glass.

4. Refrigerate for at least 1 hour or up to 3 hours. To serve, garnish each parfait with a mint sprig.

Twist It Up

This dessert is light and refreshing—perfect for summer! You can experiment with your own fruit combos, like blueberries, blackberries, peaches, kiwis, or apricots.

A NOTE FROM JACK'S MOM

When my son Jack was diagnosed with leukemia at age two, I experienced a heartache I never knew was possible. His treatment lasted a little over three years. It was a long time to deal with a life-threatening disease and all the uncertainty that goes with it. With help from our friends and family, we managed to get through it. But just one year after treatment ended, we were devastated again when his leukemia came back.

I remember being at Jack's doctor's visits, never without tissues to constantly dry my eyes. Jack would give me this half grin and tell me with clenched teeth to stop crying because it was embarrassing him! His demands would make me break down and smile as I'd answer, "I'm trying! I'm trying—it's just not in my control!" Jack was only six years old when he relapsed, but his spirits remained surprisingly good despite everything. As we left one of his appointments, Jack looked at me and his dad and said, "Look, we did this once, we can do it again!" His optimism and confidence were both striking and amazing. I tried to believe it, too, but it still wouldn't let me escape from all of my worries and anxiety as his mom.

Relapse leukemia treatment is life-changing. Everything is focused on hospital procedures, doctor's appointments, and chemo infusions. During one of Jack's hospital stays, he discovered cooking while watching the Food Network. Although we didn't know it at the time, this was an event that was going to be life-changing, too. Instead of focusing on his next hospital procedure, we focused on what new recipe we could make together when we went home. Jack's passion for cooking grew and grew, and people were inspired by his enthusiasm.

Jack finished his leukemia treatment in January 2009. Since his relapse, he has participated in numerous charity events and fund-raisers and so far has raised more than a hundred thousand dollars for pediatric cancer and leukemia research. Just as Jack dreamed, he has gotten to cook on television with Jay Leno on *The Tonight Show* and on *The Bonnie Hunt Show*, just like the celebrities he used to watch from his hospital bed. Today, Jack enjoys life to the fullest. He's not afraid to try new things or to take on new challenges. Although Jack may not be the best at something when he first tries, he perseveres and he doesn't give up. Jack and his journey have made me believe in the wonder of the world again, and that if you work hard enough and dream big enough, anything is possible.

—Lisa Witherspoon

★ ACKNOWLEDGMENTS ★

I want to thank all of my friends and family, everyone from my school at Riviera Elementary, and everyone from South Bay Brokers (where my dad works) for all of their love and support for my fund-raisers and for everything I do. I want to give a special thanks to:

Bonnie Belknap, my good friend whom I met when I was a guest on *The Bonnie Hunt Show*. Without her help and her amazing contacts in the culinary and entertainment world, I'm not sure how this book would have ever happened. I also want to thank her for the incredible food-styling work she did for me on my photo shoot. She has been a wonderful mentor.

Jim Delurgio, who helped me with my Web site. On the Fourth of July, three days before my first book deadline, my computer shut down with a huge virus. Jim came over and worked all day and through the night to rebuild my computer. He managed to save all of my data, and, miraculously, I was still able to meet my deadline. Thank you, Jim!

Michael Psaltis, my book agent, who took me on as a client even though I was only nine years old at the time and had never written a cookbook before.

Naomi Kirsten, my editor, and everyone at Chronicle Books for believing in me, my story, and recipes.

Mark and Kelly McCaslin, who let me use their beautiful home for my photo shoot. Their chef's kitchen is awesome!

Dr. Finklestein and all the nurses and fellow doctors in the Hematology and Oncology Department at Miller Children's Hospital in Long Beach, California. They have saved my life two times now! Also, I want to thank Lil Spritzer and Kaerie Ray from the Beckstrand Cancer Foundation for all their help with the promotion of this book.

I want to thank my mom and my dad for always making me feel that I could do anything I wanted to if I just set my mind to it. Also, I can't forget my brother, Josh, who is my best friend and the best recipe tester I know.

Finally, I want to thank God for always being there for me and for never letting me down even when things looked the worst. He showed me how to have faith and taught me to believe in myself. Most of all, He gave me hope so I would never give up or get discouraged. For all of this, I am so thankful!

★ INDEX ★

★ TABLE OF EQUIVALENTS ★

The exact equivalents in the following tables have been rounded for convenience.

Liquid/Dry Measurements

U.S.	METRIC
1/4 teaspoon	1.25 milliliters
1/2 teaspoon	2.5 milliliters
1 teaspoon	5 milliliters
1 tablespoon (3 teaspoons)	15 milliliters
1 fluid ounce (2 tablespoons)	30 milliliters
1/4 cup	60 milliliters
1/3 cup	80 milliliters
1/2 cup	120 milliliters
1 cup	240 milliliters
1 pint (2 cups)	480 milliliters
1 quart (4 cups, 32 ounces)	960 milliliters
1 gallon (4 quarts, 64 ounces)	3.84 liters
1 ounce (by weight)	28 grams
1 pound	448 grams
2.2 pounds	1 kilogram

Lengths

U.S.	METRIC
1/8 inch	3 millimeters
1/4 inch	6 millimeters
1/2 inch	12 millimeters
1 inch	2.5 centimeters

Oven Temperature

FAHRENHEIT	CELSIUS	GAS
250	120	1/2
275	140	1
300	150	2
325	160	3
350	180	4
375	190	5
400	200	6
425	220	7
450	230	8
475	240	9
500	260	10